RELIGION
at the
ISLES OF SHOALS

Anglicans, Puritans, Missionaries,
UUs (Unitarian Universalists), and
UCCs (United Church of Christ)

BY
LOIS WILLIAMS

ILLUSTRATIONS BY
BOBBY WILLIAMS

FOREWORD BY
THE REVEREND BRADFORD GREELEY

PETER E. RANDALL PUBLISHER LLC
PORTSMOUTH, NEW HAMPSHIRE
2006

© 2006 Star Island Corporation

Additional copies are available from:
    Star Island Corporation
    10 Vaughan Mall, Suite 8
    Portsmouth NH 03801
    www.starisland.org
    603-430-6272

ISBN: 0-9742414-0-7

Library of Congress Control Number: 2005935026

Produced by
Peter E. Randall Publisher LLC
PO Box 4726, Portsmouth NH 03802
www.perpublisher.com

Front Cover photograph by Bobby Williams

Contents

Foreword

For those of us who grew up believing that the Pilgrims and the *Mayflower* defined New England culture and religion, finding out otherwise can come as quite a surprise. We learned about the perilous voyage across the North Atlantic in the late fall. We were told about the miraculous piles of gathered and covered corn they helped themselves to. We heard about the abundant fish and game that saved the lives of those hardy non-conformists who braved such hazards in order to practice their religion freely.

What a shock it is to learn that well before those intrepid voyagers made their way to our side of the salt sea, British fishermen lived on the islands off the coast of Maine and New Hampshire year-round, filling boats that arrived in summer and winter with dried fish for sale in England. These men had befriended the Natives, built stockades and houses, and started settling on the mainland at the same time the Pilgrims arrived. These entrepreneurs brought business to the New World and established churches.

Lois Williams has studied one of the oldest and longest standing of the island fishing stations. She traces the religious history of the Isles of Shoals from its earliest development through four hundred years of evolution and change. Williams is well suited to the task. She has been researching her family's antecedents of Plymouth Colony, and it was an obvious detour to the Isles of Shoals and the very beginnings of Protestant religion north of Plymouth.

The story is replete with episodes of the conflict that marked the existence of both the Anglican and the Puritan churches in the area and, sadly, the conflict between the powers of religion and the dissenters. The fortunes of the Shoals waxed and waned in the centuries that followed, depending on the fishing trade, the Navigation Acts, and wars. With Lois Williams's history, we learn about the lives and contributions of the clergy who ministered to the islands' inhabitants.

For those who have seen the Isles of Shoals or visited them, whether once for a few hours or for weeks over many years, this book tells a wonderful story and brings to life the drama of what prepared the way for today. For those who want to understand more about the life and development of the Isles of Shoals, this book includes a compendium of references that will gladden the heart of any student. For those who have a few hours to expand their appreciation of the role religion plays in maintaining life and community on a small chunk of rock seven miles out to sea, this book provides rich insights.

Reverend Bradford Greeley
Portsmouth, New Hampshire
July 2005

The Isles of Shoals

Religion has been integral to 365 years of Isles of Shoals history–under Anglican clergy in the mid-seventeenth century, Puritan preachers through the eighteenth century, and missionaries "propagating the gospel" in the nineteenth century. Early twentieth century summers brought Unitarians (now Unitarian Universalists) and Congregationalists (now the United Church of Christ), who are still coming to the Star Island Religious and Educational Conference Center at the Isles of Shoals.

Writing in *The Isles of Shoals* in 1873, John Scribner Jenness noted the fine climate that made these islands off Portsmouth "the most frequented and perhaps the most fashionable summer resort in New England." While Boston and Portland experience "cheerless fogs and mists and soaking rains," wrote Jenness, the Portsmouth area, equidistant from each, "rejoices in clear skies and gentle breezes." Long before the summer resort era, these same clear skies and gentle breezes brought the first men to the Isles of Shoals to fish and dry their catch.

Four centuries ago, English fishermen undertook annual voyages to Georges Bank in the southern Gulf of Maine—historically among the richest fishing grounds in the world. Georges Bank is an offshore underwater plateau rising from the deep Atlantic, and at fifteen feet below sea level, it is shallow enough that sunlight penetrates to sea bottom and photosynthesis nourishes the underwater vegetation that is home to bottom-feeding cod. The cold Georges Bank waters are rich in oxygen, untouched by the warm current of the Gulf Stream which runs farther offshore in deep water, and Maine's rivers continually replenish the waters of Georges Bank with the detritus and small organisms on which fish feed.

A century before English fishermen came to Georges Bank, Portuguese, Spaniards, and Frenchmen were fishing the Grand Banks off Newfoundland. Salt was readily available in southern Europe and the Iberians were "wet" fishermen—that is, every member of the crew fished from the anchored ship and filled barrels with heavily salted fish. But salt was at a premium in the British Isles, so the "dry" fishermen of England sailed with a shipboard crew who fished and extra men who were put ashore. The shore crew gutted and lightly salted the catch and spread split fish on raised platforms, called flakes, to dry in the sun.

Unlike the Newfoundland fisheries, which had a single summer fishing season, Georges Bank enjoyed a summer and a winter fish run, and Englishmen began to live year-round on the Shoals to fish both seasons. Fish caught at the Isles of Shoals, wrote Jenness, were "larger and finer than those brought from the Banks of Newfoundland," and the "dry and salubrious atmosphere" of the Shoals was more favorable than that of the mainland. The Shoals "invited settlement, merely by the advantages they furnished for fishery." Centrally located to the first settlements on New England's rocky northern coast, and with deep-water access sufficient for sailing ships of the day, the Isles of Shoals became a center of fisheries and coastal trade.

The chance for trade and profit brought a handful of nominally Anglican settlers to the northern New England coast. The phrase "We came to fish" figured in the lore of many Maine and New Hampshire settlements, sometimes recalled as "We came to fish, not to pray." In contrast, religious motivation brought fourteen thousand Puritans to the Massachusetts Bay Colony during the period of the Great Migration from 1630 to 1642. In 1630, a fleet of eleven ships sailed to Boston Harbor with the first of the Puritans, led by John Winthrop. The fleet's flagship passed the Isles of Shoals, already an established fishing station, where Winthrop "saw a ship lie there at anchor, and five or six shallops under sail."

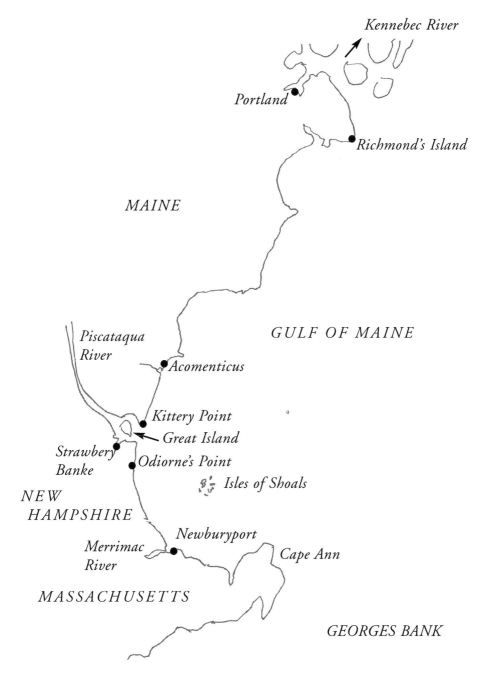

Kennebec River

Portland

Richmond's Island

MAINE

GULF OF MAINE

Piscataqua River

Acomenticus

Kittery Point

Great Island

Strawbery Banke

Odiorne's Point

Isles of Shoals

NEW HAMPSHIRE

Merrimac River

Newburyport

Cape Ann

MASSACHUSETTS

GEORGES BANK

THE UPPER NEW ENGLAND COAST

Beginnings of New Hampshire and Maine

King James I of England granted a royal charter in 1606 to two companies of Knights, Gentlemen, Merchants and other Adventurers, authorizing them to plant colonies in England's North American territory. The wealthier London Company underwrote the 1608 Jamestown settlers and backed the Pilgrims in 1620. The smaller Plymouth Company in 1607 sponsored Popham, a short-lived settlement at the mouth of Maine's Kennebec River, which was the first attempt to establish an English colony in New England. Both the Virginia Company and the Plymouth Company sent vessels to the coast of Maine to bring home fish and furs, and independent fishermen continued to ply the waters of the Gulf of Maine.

It was the Plymouth Company that licensed Captain John Smith's voyage to explore the northern coast in 1614. Smith mapped the New England coastline, identified the "safe harbor and rocky shore" at the mouth of the Piscataqua River, and saw the Isles of Shoals, "a heap together, none near them," naming them Smyth's Isles. Smith returned to England with a cargo of fish and furs, heightening interest in the profitability of fisheries and the fur trade. Sir Fernando Gorges reorganized the Plymouth group in 1620 as the "Council . . . for the Planting, Ruling, and Governing of New England in America"—the first use of New England as a name for the area. The Plymouth Council obtained a charter from King James with rights to trade, colonize, and tax fishermen "in the adjoining seas of New England"—the "odious fishery monopoly."

The monopoly, wrote Jenness, was intended as a revenue source for the Crown, with "a charge of five pounds sterling upon every thirty tons of shipping engaged in the American fisheries." William D. Williamson's 1832 *History of Maine*, one of the area's earliest histories, tells that the Plymouth Council commissioned an admiral of New England and sent him to "restrain all unlicensed ships from fishing and trade" and "exact of all interlopers, payment of penal sums prescribed." The admiral found the fishermen at the Shoals and at Monhegan and Pemaquid on the coast "too sturdy and stubborn for him to control," wrote Jenness.

Puritans in the House of Commons chose to contest as "a public grievance" the king's power to grant exclusive privileges to royal corporations—an opening maneuver to England's religiously motivated Civil War 20 years later. King James insisted on his royal prerogative, and, with the House of Lords, backed Gorges in his defense of the council monopoly. The House leader challenged Gorges: "If you, alone, are to pack and dry fish, you attempt a monopoly of the wind and sun." The House repealed the monopoly, but King James countered by dissolving Parliament in 1622 and sending its leaders to the Tower, leaving the monopoly still in effect. English Puritans fought the monopoly again in 1625, and King Charles I similarly "refused to yield a little of his prerogative." Although the Plymouth Council gave up its fishing monopoly soon afterward, the "free fisheries" issue was an early instance of Parliament's efforts to assert supreme authority over the colonies in America.

Under the Plymouth Council's charter, Sir Fernando and Captain John Mason claimed land between the Merrimac and Kennebec Rivers and issued land grants to others to encourage settlement. With a later additional grant of land in northern New England, Gorges and Mason founded the Laconia Company. The company set up fur-trading stations along rivers to tap the rich fur country, and established coastal settlements for fishing and farming. By 1633 the Laconia Company charter had been dissolved, but outposts were in place at Great Island (now New Castle) at the mouth of the Piscataqua River, Strawbery Banke (now Portsmouth) two miles upstream, and the Isles of Shoals. Jenness wrote, "During the existence of the Company of Laconia, both the Island and the mainland had become peopled with considerable numbers of laborers of all sorts, and permanent buildings had been erected," and by 1640, "this little cluster of bare rocks . . . was a chief fishing station in the Gulf of Maine."

Reaching the end of their deep pockets with little to show for their investments, Gorges and Mason divided their holdings in 1635. They drew a line at the Piscataqua River, extending the division out to sea through the Isles of Shoals—still the dividing line between New Hampshire and Maine. Captain Mason held land between the Merrimac and Piscataqua Rivers, and the Shoals islands of Star, Londoners (now Lunging), White, and Seavey. Sir Fernando held land between the Piscataqua and Kennebec Rivers, and the Shoals islands of Hog (now Appledore), Smutty Nose (at one time Church Island, later Haley Island, and now Smuttynose), Malaga, Cedar, and Duck. Gorges and Mason never saw their lands across the sea, where they were said to have invested three times the profits returned to them.

Duck Island

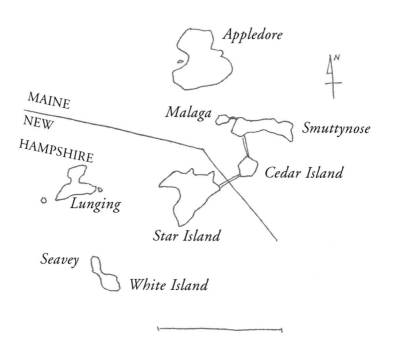

Appledore

N

MAINE

NEW

HAMPSHIRE

Malaga

Smuttynose

Cedar Island

Lunging

Star Island

Seavey

White Island

ISLES OF SHOALS

Anglicans and Puritans in England

The political and religious rebellion in Europe resulting in the separation of the Protestant churches from what we now know as the Roman Catholic Church has come to be called the Reformation—the name signaled the reforming intent of new church leadership. In 1517, Martin Luther protested corrupt practices of the Christian church in western Europe, particularly that of buying eternal salvation through the purchase of indulgences. Luther eliminated the church calendar of saints' days, banished church ornamentation as "idolatry," and confiscated the property and wealth of religious orders. Proclaiming the Bible the only source of God's word, Luther translated the Bible into German in 1534, and the printing press soon made vernacular Bibles available to Protestants everywhere. Seeing congregational singing as an important communal experience, Luther composed hymns still sung today, including "A Mighty Fortress Is Our God." Lutheranism became the religion of northern Germany and Scandinavia.

In Switzerland, Ulrich Zwingli, John Calvin, and others further "reformed" church practices while contesting Luther's interpretation of many points as well as the interpretations of each other. Calvin's writings developed the doctrine of predestination: An all-knowing God determines each man's eternal destiny, with salvation for the few whom God elects and everlasting torment for the rest. While Calvin himself opposed singing non-biblical texts in church, Geneva became a center of church music. Reformed Protestantism—not yet called Calvinism—spread through much of western Europe as the Reformed Church, into Scotland as the Presbyterian Church, and to followers in France (the Huguenots).

Southern Europeans remained loyal to their church, then loosely centered in Rome. Many forces converged to bring about changes that strengthened the church, codified at the decade-long Council of Trent, which ended in 1563, and resulting in the Counter-Reformation. Tritentine reforms led to a more centralized church, greater uniformity of practice, and clarity on theological issues. Before the Council of Trent and long before Protestants began to look to distant lands, Portuguese and Spanish missionary efforts were bringing conquered peoples in Central and South American and on the fringes of Africa and Asia into the Catholic Church.

The Church of England dated from King Henry VIII's break with the Roman Catholic Church and the 1534 Act of Supremacy, which recognized the king of England as the head of the Church of England. For a time, the ideas of the continent's Protestant reformers gained ground in England and influenced early Anglican prayer books. Soon, though, Queen Elizabeth I curbed reformers within the Church of England with the 1559 Acts of Uniformity and Supremacy and a more conservative Book of Common Prayer. Theologically, Elizabeth's Anglican Church was a modified Calvinism, but Anglicanism largely retained Roman Catholic practices— hierarchical governance, liturgical worship, and the ceremonialism of choirs, altar cloths, and priestly vestments.

Even before the Elizabethan period, English reformers seeking to "purify" the church came to be called Puritans, and Puritan thought took root among middle-class townspeople in eastern England. English Protestants worked with Calvin in Geneva to produce the Geneva Bible in 1560, widely used by the Puritans for two hundred years. Puritans retained the Calvinist theology of the Church of England, but differed with Anglicans on church doctrine, church governance, and worship, and, like other dissent- ing groups, held their own services. Puritans believed that salvation was only for the elect, focused on a preaching ministry, and limited church member- ship to those publicly professing a profound spiritual experience, called *conversion*. Puritans also took issue with what they saw as the hedonism of the English people, and looked to build a society of religious and moral virtue.

Four centuries ago, as Englishmen were planting the first settlements in the New World, religious issues increasingly divided the English homeland. During this period of theological controversy, King James I came to the throne in 1603. In an effort to unify England—and to supersede what he saw as the seditious Geneva Bible—James appointed 54 translators, drawn from both Anglican and Puritan scholars of the day, to produce the King James Bible. Royal rapprochement with the Puritans was, however, short-lived.

Over time, some groups left the Church of England as Separatists, including the Pilgrims. In contrast, Puritans remained within the Anglican Church, believing it a true church although corrupted. King Charles I dismissed Parliament in 1629 and sanctioned persecution of Puritans, and an exodus of Puritans to New England began in 1630. Still considering themselves members of the Church of England, Puritans of the Massachusetts Bay Colony sought to establish a temporal and ecclesiastical form of government that would be a godly society and an example to the mother country. Although not leaving England as Separatists, the Puritans' separation from England by the Atlantic Ocean in time effected their separation from the Church of England.

The English Parliament revolted against the authority of King Charles I in 1642, and with the help of Scottish Presbyterians, the largely Puritan Parliamentarians (Roundheads) battled Anglican Cavaliers in the English Civil War. Charles I surrendered to Parliament in 1646, only to be beheaded by the Roundheads in 1648. Oliver Cromwell, and later his son, governed with increasing chaos as lord protector of the English Commonwealth. The war ended with restoration of the monarchy in 1660: The Royalists were again in power, King Charles II came to the English throne, and Anglicanism was once more the state church.

Puritans and Presbyterians were allies against the Cavaliers during the English Civil War. The groups were in agreement on their adherence to Calvinism and opposition to Anglicanism but differed on the issue of church governance, with the Presbyterians retaining a modification of the Anglican structure of local churches supervised by layers of centralized leadership groups. Each Puritan group, on the other hand, was an independent and self-governing congregation that chose and ordained its own minister, and the term *congregationalist* was coming into use to describe Puritan churches. Puritan churches in England were called Congregational, although that would not be a New World church name during the colonial period, when Puritanism was the established church, or "standing order," in New England.

Anglicans at the Isles of Shoals

The colonial New Englanders we know most about were Puritans. As explained by Charles A. Hazlett in the 1915 *History of Rockingham County, New Hampshire*, "Until recent times the history of New England has been written exclusively by men who, though no doubt meaning to be fair-minded, were either Puritan themselves, or strongly imbued with the Puritan prejudice." Yet, Jenness noted, during the earliest years of Portsmouth and the Isles of Shoals—when the area was busier than Boston Harbor—"the founders of the Isles of Shoals, like those of Maine and New Hampshire in general, felt little sympathy with the religious tenets of New Plymouth and Massachusetts."

It was clearly part of the Gorges and Mason plan that their New World settlements would be Anglican. "His great preference," Hazlett wrote of Gorges, was for colonization "by sons of Episcopacy rather than those withdrawn from its protection and rewards." King Charles's 1639 charter to Gorges granted him "full power, license, and authority to build and erect . . . churches and chapels . . . and consecrate the same according to all ecclesiastical laws" of England. Mason's will bequeathed one thousand acres "toward the maintenance of an honest, godly, and religious preacher of God's word" in New Hampshire and "a flagon and cloths for the communion table."

Early Anglican clergymen on the northern coast served settlers at Odiorne's Point (near the mouth of the Piscataqua River) and New Castle in what is now New Hampshire, along with Saco Bay (near Portland) and Accominticus (now York) in what is now Maine. Williamson called the brick meetinghouse built about 1640 on Smuttynose Island "possibly the first in the province;" the brick would have come from England as ship ballast. Early histories differ on whether there was also a church on Hog Island, home to the largest group of Shoalers.

Although there was no resident clergyman at the Shoals, the Anglican concept of parish included all within its boundaries, and mainland clergy reached out to fishermen on the Isles of Shoals. The Reverend Joseph Hull, an early Church of England clergyman at York, before 1640 occasionally visited the islands where he "preached and administered the Holy

Sacraments." Jenness wrote, "In this Hull ran little risk of being disciplined, for he lived in the province of Maine which stoutly supported Episcopalian and royalist friends." The next year, the Reverend Richard Gibson, by then at York, held services at the Shoals. Early Anglican clergy traveled far to minister to those in the outer reaches of a parish, and the Reverend Robert Jordan, an Anglican minister at Richmond's Island (now Cape Elizabeth, near Portland, Maine), also held services in 1640 at the Shoals, a fifty-mile sail from his parish at Casco Bay. These Anglican clergymen—the Reverends Hull, Gibson, and Jordan—soon ran afoul of expanding Puritanism.

Anglicans and Puritans on New England's Northern Coast

Pilgrims and Puritans carried their aversion to the Church of England to the New World. Even before the coming of the Puritans, Pilgrims expelled an Anglican from Plymouth, sending him to the Isles of Shoals, where he was held until he could be put aboard a ship sailing to England. As described by Jenness, "Thomas Morton, one of the first victims of the intolerance of the Pilgrim Fathers, was, in 1628, banished from New England in a vessel, which sailed from these Islands . . . One of his chief sins proven seems to have been a mirthful and sportive temper, and the evidence of it was that he and his merry men were guilty of dancing around a Maypole . . . and of composing a profane, licentious song."

The Puritans took control of New Hampshire in 1640, targeting its Anglican clergy as representing a link with the British Crown and driving the Reverend Richard Gibson from his Anglican parish at Strawbery Banke. Reverend Gibson moved to York and then in 1642 took refuge at the Isles of Shoals, where, ignoring the Puritans, Shoalers welcomed the Anglican Gibson as their first settled minister. After a year at the Shoals, Puritan authorities seized Gibson as he was passing through Boston, but because Gibson was on his way to England, he was released. John Winthrop wrote that Reverend Gibson "this year was entertained by the fishermen of the Isle of Shoals to preach to them. He being wholly addicted to the hierarchy and discipline of England, did exercise a ministerial function in the same way and did marry and baptize at the Isle of Shoals." Winthrop accused Gibson of "opposing Massachusetts title to those parts and provoking the people to revolt."

The Massachusetts Bay Colony continued its expansion northward into Maine. Puritans censured Reverend Hooker of Richmond's Island, forbidding him to perform the Anglican sacraments of marriage and baptism. In 1654 and again in 1663, the Puritans arrested Hooker and jailed him in Boston for continuing to administer the rites of the Church of England, and Winthrop charged that he, too, "provoked the people of the Isles of Shoals to revolt against the government." Reverend Hooker's baptismal font is now in the collections of the Maine Historical Society in Portland.

In time, persecution of the clergy of one denomination by the authorities of another played out near the Isles of Shoals in a different manner. The Massachusetts Bay Colony lost New Hampshire in 1679, when Charles II arbitrarily established New Hampshire as a separate royal province. Two years later, the king appointed a New Hampshire governor and lieutenant government who saw Puritanism, and especially its ministers, as fostering seditious thought and thwarting the plans of the Crown. The Reverend Joshua Moody, Portsmouth's eminent Puritan clergyman and leader of a people "devout and tenacious of their worship," was outspoken in his opposition to reestablishment of the Church of England in New Hampshire. Lieutenant Governor Cranfield, an Anglican, ordered Moody to administer the sacrament of communion to him "as it was done in the Church of England." As expected, Reverend Moody refused. He was arrested, tried, and jailed for thirteen weeks, and banned from further preaching in New Hampshire.

The Reverend John Brock

Ten years after becoming part of the Massachusetts Bay Colony, "Shoalers could no longer maintain the attitude of resistance," wrote Jenness, and Massachusetts "brought the entire Shoals group into a condition of nominal obedience." In 1650, the Massachusetts governor sent "a sound Puritan divine" to establish Puritanism among the Shoalers for the political end of strengthening the authority of Massachusetts. Brock was "the first of a long line of Congregational ministers who rendered noble and self-sacrificing service until the settlement went down in hopeless decay." Celia Thaxter later wrote of Reverend Brock, "All that we hear of this man is so fine, he is represented as having been so faithful, zealous, intelligent, and humane, that it is no wonder the community flourished while he sat at the helm."

Brock kept a journal for part of his life—not noticed until about 1940, and excerpted and published in 1944 in *American Antiquities* as "The Autobiographical Memoranda of John Brock, 1636–1659." Brock had followed each of his journal statements with extended religious speculation, but "Memoranda" editors omitted this material. Brock's summary of his years before leaving England caught the essence of the Puritan cause:

> God helpt me to see the Evil of the Idolatrous Worship &
> Ceremonies of the Church of England . . . I was encouraged . . . to
> love the Saints that were called Puritans. Persecutors grew daily more
> odious in their Ways . . . The Lord . . . heard me to open a Way for us
> to leave England & get to the Society of a beloved Christian.

Brock and his parents came from England to the Massachusetts Bay Colony in 1638, settling in Dedham, and Brock entered Harvard in 1643. After graduation, Brock "kept school" in Rowley and began preaching as an assistant to the minister. In 1649 he wrote, "The College . . . would have me go to the Charibdee (Caribbean) Islands . . . but the News of the Wickedness of the People takes away my Heart." Instead, in the phrase of church records, "Brock was settled at the Shoals from 1650 to 1662."

Since there was no town at the Shoals, the requirement that a town provide a house for its minister was not applicable, so Brock boarded with various families. Each family must have considered the extra mouth to feed an imposition, and made its boarder less than welcome. Brock's journal recorded dissatisfaction with each lodging and anxiety about the next:

[1652] I am about to change my Habitation. The People are not so good, where I have been.
[1654] I know not where I shall winter.
[1656] I know not how to live here another Year, unless some Providence may appear to my comfort.
[1659] I am held in a strait for the Present in Regard of my comfortable Being this winter.

Brock wrote of his frustration as religious leader of the Shoalers and was anxious to leave, but his journal reflected the Islanders' growing appreciation of their preacher, and hinted at economic issues at the Shoals—the precariousness of the fish catch and swindling "Traders."

[1651] My Life is not comfortable through some troublesome Spirits; but I shall overcome them with Goodness. Everywhere my poor Preaching is blessed.
[1652] The Hand of God is much against us in our Fishing. My people have not Breathings after Goodness . . . There is a great want of Discretion in some Men's Trading . . . Growth of Grace is very slow.
[1653] I have had more Experience of the Affections of my People towards me. Methinks that the Providence of God doth lead me to tarry with mine another year. My People give me Encouragement to God's Praise.
[1654] My people do not appear to be settled . . . The People begin to seal their Hearts again. Fishing is much weakened this season . . . We have our Trials in this Wilderness, in all respects. God will find out the Sins of Traders, amongst us.
[1656] My People can not endure to hear that I should leave them . . . I hope it shall be for the better that I stay with the Islanders.

Brock stopped writing in his journal in 1659 and left the Shoals in 1662, accepting a call from the First Parish of Wakefield, Massachusetts. Brock was ordained by the Wakefield congregation, married the deceased minister's widow, and had a home of his own at last. This was an era when a congregational call and ordination meant a permanent position, barring congregational dissatisfaction and dismissal of its clergyman, and Brock remained at Wakefield until his death in 1688.

The Reverend Cotton Mather wrote the massive *Magnalia Christi American*—in English, *Ecclesiastical History of New England*—and subtitled "from its first planting, in the year 1620, unto the year of Our Lord 1698." The *Magnalia* remains a useful record of colonial history despite Mather's extensive sermonizing. Mather structured the *Magnalia* as a series of biographies, and his section on graduates of Harvard University begins with Reverend Brock. Isles of Shoals historians often quote Cotton Mather as saying of Brock, "He dwelt as near heaven as any man on earth." Indeed, Mather used these words, but in the context of Brock's ministry at Wakefield. Mather wrote about Brock's work at the Isles of Shoals in words that were more relevant: "Here a spiritual fisherman did more than a little good among a rude company of literal ones."

In an era when miracles were seen as important evidence of God's work, Mather attributed a number of "cures" to Reverend Brock. Mather's "miracle" of interest to Shoals history relates to an incident that took place while Brock was at Wakefield—the imprisonment of Reverend Josiah Moody for refusing to follow Anglican rites:

> One who then lived with Mr. Brock, seeing him one morning very sorrowful, ask'd him the reason of his present sorrow. Said he, "I am very troubled for my dear Brother Moody, who is imprisoned by Canfield, but I will this day seek to the Lord on his behalf, and I believe my God will hear me!" And on that very day was Mr. Moody (forty miles off) by a marvelous disposal of Providence, delivered out of his imprisonment.

Most writers of Shoals history have repeated word-for-word Reverend Brock's sermon about fishermen missing a worship service. The "fish story" likely originated with Mather, and as with much of Mather's writing, was more sermonizing than history. Mather painted Brock as a Christlike figure among his fishermen:

> When Mr. Brock lived in the Isle of Shoals, he brought the people into an agreement that, besides the Lord's-days, they would spend one day every month together in the worship of our Lord Jesus Christ. On a certain day, which by their agreement belong'd unto the exercises of religion, being arrived, the fishermen came to Mr. Brock, and asked him that they might put by the meeting, and go a fishing, because they had lost many days by the foulness of the weather. He, seeing that without and against his consent they resolved upon doing what they had asked of him, replied, "If you will go away, I say unto you, catch fish,

if you can! But as for you that will tarry, and worship the Lord Jesus Christ this day, I will pray until Him for you, that you may take fish till you are weary." Thirty men went away from the meeting, and five tarried. The thirty which went away from the meeting, with all their skill, could catch but four fishes; the five which tarried, went forth afterwards, and they took five hundred. The fishermen after this readily attended whatever meetings Mr. Brock appointed them.

Writing in *Among the Isles of Shoals* two centuries later, Celia Thaxter recalled an incident when, thinking it was Sunday, she asked a young Star Islander who had come to the Laighton cottage, " 'Well, Jud, how many fish have they caught today at Star?' Jud looked askance and answered, like one who did not wish to be trifled with, 'We don't go a-fishing Sundays!' " Similarly, John Downs's 1941 memoir of his childhood at the Isles of Shoals, *Sprays of Salt*, recorded "a superstition" that persisted through the nineteenth century: "If fishermen had not gone to worship at the regular service on Sunday, they could not expect to get a big haul of fish during the week."

The Reverend Joseph Hull moved to the islands in 1663 to follow the Reverend Brock. Hall died in 1665 without receiving his expected payment of twenty pounds from the Shoalers. Jenness credited the Reverend Hull with trying to find common ground with both Anglicans and Puritans, and the Shoalers seem to have welcomed his more tolerant approach. Jenness, himself an Episcopalian, saw the early New Hampshire people as "thorough-paced Episcopalians," although that would not be the name of the Anglican Church in America until after the Revolutionary War.

Jenness noted the Anglican Church's "genial patronage of gaiety and merriment" and the Prayer Book "supplying, ready always for use, a beautiful liturgy," in contrast to the "sour austerities of the Reformers" and "intellectual vexations that tormented the dissenters," as he put it. "The deeper mysteries of religion were utterly incomprehensible to our ignorant fishermen; the subtle distinctions between sanctification and justification, between the covenant of works and the covenant of faith, which employed the pulpits of the Puritans, were to the people of the Shoals the dreariest jargon."

FISHING SHALLOP

"The Wealthiest Settlement in the New World"

While Celia Thaxter attributed the prosperity of the Shoals to Reverend Brock's influence and Williamson to the "industry, intelligence, and pure morals" of the original settlers, economic forces favored opportunistic entrepreneurs and made the Shoals, in Lyman V. Rutledge's words, "the wealthiest settlement in the New World." According to Jenness, "Not only were vast quantities of fish taken and cured by the fishermen of the Islands, but the harbor became the entrepot for the fish caught in other parts of the Gulf of Maine, and thence exported" to southern Europe and the Caribbean Islands, "bringing rich return cargoes of wine, sugar, tobacco, etc., which were distributed from the warehouses of the traders at the Shoals and Strawbery Banke." These were the "Traders" of Brock's journal.

Jenness continued, "The estates of the leading men at this period . . . were among the largest in New England." Private fortunes made at the Shoals allowed William Pepperell; the brothers Richard, William, and John Cutt; and others to move to Kittery or Portsmouth, where they built bigger warehouses, expanded business enterprises, and lived in grand houses. The Pepperells amassed a fortune, and John and Richard Cutt were the largest landowners in Portsmouth in the 1660s, with John Cutt becoming the first provincial president of New Hampshire in 1680.

With the Navigation Acts of 1651 and 1660, England moved to restrict shipping to and from its colonies to vessels built in England or the colonies—"English bottoms"—and to have all commerce to and from the colonies pass through English ports. The 1660 act was immediately modified, justified in its preamble because "merchants trading for New England find themselves much grieved." The change permitted fish and "other rough commodities" to go directly to where they "better vend." Fish could thus be shipped from New England to "Catholic Europe," as it was then known, without stopping in England, although the requirement for English bottoms still held.

Dunfish, made by alternately "sweating" fish in eelgrass and salt hay and drying the fish on racks in the sun, was a specialty of the Isles of Shoals, and highly valued in Spain and Portugal. In Europe, wrote Jenness, Shoals fish brought "three or four times" the price of fish from Newfoundland fisheries, and flakes (fish racks) were part of the Star Island scene through 1870. Celia Thaxter wrote, "From three to four thousand quintals [one hundred kilograms] of fish were yearly caught and cured by the islanders; and, beside their trade with Spain, large quantities of fish were also carried to Portsmouth for the West India market." By the Revolutionary War, one third of New England's fish exports went to southern Europe and two thirds to the West Indies, where its lowest grade of fish fed slaves.

Hog Island was then the center of the Shoals population. Rutledge's guidebook to the Isles of Shoals, *Ten Miles Out*, noted the site of an early academy for boys, "well known and patronized by citizens of the mainland" but now "discernible only as field boulders following the lines of old foundations." Shoals leaders petitioned Massachusetts for town or township status for the islands. Their application was originally refused on the grounds that there were "few or no . . . members of the established Puritan Church in good standing," although township status was later granted.

For the two decades from 1661 to 1681, the Shoals in their entirety constituted the township of Appledore, first under the jurisdiction of Massachusetts, then of New Hampshire, and eventually of Maine, which was still part of the Massachusetts Bay Colony. Massachusetts Bay formalized its power in Maine by buying out the heirs of Sir Fernando Gorges in 1677. Maine would remain under the administration of Massachusetts as the Territory of Maine until long after the Revolutionary War, becoming the state of Maine in 1820. Shoalers had sought township status, but they resisted its concomitant taxation and gathered at the brick church on Smuttynose. According to Jenness:

> When the Massachusetts authorities, in 1677, undertook to collect a little something toward the expenses of Government, the Shoalers flew into open rebellion . . . Henry Joslyn climbed up to the belfry of the meetinghouse and rang the alarm; people ran together in the church . . . and it was solemnly declared that they would not pay a penny unless the Governor and Council would guarantee that money raised should be "laid out upon the Isles of Shoals."

Soon afterward, in 1679, Massachusetts Bay Colony lost control of New Hampshire and the Isles of Shoals were split between New Hampshire and Maine, retaining the Mason and Gorges line of division. In a mass migration in 1679 and 1680, forty Hog Island families moved across

Gosport Harbor to Star Island in New Hampshire. Shoalers were avoiding the town taxes of Kittery, Maine, as well as the rigid ways of the Massachusetts authorities. Celia Thaxter surmised, "Probably the greater advantages of landing and the convenience of a wide cove at the entrance of the village, with a little harbor where the fishing-craft might anchor with some security, were also inducements."

Hog Island, once a community of eighty houses, was deserted, and Maine dissolved the Township of Appledore in 1681—there would not be local government at the Shoals again for thirty-five years. Maine still had jurisdiction over the sparsely populated Hog Island, however, as well as over Smuttynose, with its deteriorating brick church. In 1685, Maine Shoalers were called before the York County Court "for their neglect in not maintaining a sufficient meeting house for the worship of God," but Shoalers ignored the summons.

The move to Star Island came as the prosperity of the Shoals was waning, and it was no longer the center of fishing and shipping that it once had been. "Hardly a single one of the ancient family names remained," Jenness wrote, and Shoals "business and wealth had fallen principally into the hands of three chief proprietors . . . who resided in Massachusetts, and carried on the fisheries at the Shoals by means of 'thirdsmen' as they were called."

An appendix in Jenness's book describes the changed demographics of the Shoals. After threats of an attack by Indians in 1690 and a later fear of attack by the French sailing from Canada, islanders petitioned Massachusetts for "forty sufficient soldiers fit for service, whose charge both for meat, drink, and wages we will at our own cost freely disburse and discharge." Forty soldiers were sent to the Shoals in 1693, but the promised wages, food, and lodgings were not forthcoming. In a communication to the governor, the troop's commander described the Shoalers: "Some of them [the thirdsmen] have no families here [and] come from the mainland to avoid all public service and support" for the war. "Others have families here [but] plead much poverty." The commander noted that Star Island's three major landowners lived in Ipswich and Boston, but "will not give any assistance, though they have estates, boats and servants here."

The First Star Island Meetinghouse

For a time after Hull's death in 1665, there was no preaching at the Shoals. Although the Puritans of Massachusetts Bay Colony had sent Brock to the Shoals on behalf of both church and state, theologically Puritanism was not an evangelizing religion, except for its missionary work among Native Americans. As the growing number of Harvard graduates sought positions for which they were educated, the pool of men prepared for the ministry grew faster than the number of congregations seeking ministers. Many ministerial hopefuls went to preach in an unchurched community, hoping to lead a group to "gathering a church" and ordaining their leader. The term *preached at _*, as in "preached at the Shoals," usually meant a non-ordained man in the pulpit. Alternatively, as in Brock's case, becoming known as a powerful preacher could bring a call from an established church in need of a minister, and ordination there.

The Reverend Samuel Belcher studied for the ministry at Harvard. On graduation, he came to the Shoals—a 1671 deed for property on Smuttynose described it as bounded "East and south by house and land of Mr. Belcher." Belcher preached at the Isles of Shoals for twenty-three years, from 1669 to 1692, when "ill health obliged him to leave that place." Belcher later preached in West Newbury and died seventeen years after he left the Shoals. Though he was never ordained, Reverend Belcher was remembered as "a good scholar, a judicious divine, a holy and humble man."

Under the leadership of Reverend Belcher, Star Islanders built their first meetinghouse, "a substantial structure of wood" 28 feet wide and 48 feet long (somewhat larger than the later stone chapel) and "on a lofty point of Star Island" sixty feet above low tide. Islanders funded its construction, with most outlays in labor rather than in cash. Trees never grew to any size at the Shoals, and either this meetinghouse or its successor, also of wood, was built with timber salvaged from a wrecked Spanish ship. Today's visitors to the chapel can see the sign that long had been above the chapel door, now hung inside for protection against further weathering: "Originally constructed of the timbers from the wreck of a Spanish ship, A.D. 1685."

The Spanish ship must have crashed on Shoals rocks shortly before construction of the meetinghouse—driftwood cast ashore was the Shoalers' major fuel, and ship's timbers of an earlier wreck would have long since been burned. Although the requirement to "ship in English bottoms" still held, an exception was made in the Navigation Act of 1663 for "salt for the fisheries of New England and Newfoundland." The Spanish ship was likely bringing salt for use by the Shoals fishermen; the salt pans and other saltworks of early settlers yielded little in New England's short summers and cold climate, and the fisheries relied on salt from the Iberian Peninsula.

It also may have been that the Spanish ship carried smugglers. Smuggling was rampant at the Shoals as well as all along the coast of British America— smugglers were evading both British duties on imports and the requirement for shipping in English vessels. Much later, in 1813, another Spanish ship wrecked at the Shoals, remembered by the graves of its sailors on Smuttynose and in Celia Thaxter's poem "The Spaniards' Graves."

Like other early American meetinghouses built in the deliberately plain style of English and northern Protestant churches of the time, Star Island's meetinghouse would have had stark interiors, clear windows, and a blunt tower. The steeple so prominent in later church architecture was not yet a feature of the religious buildings of dissenting groups. Writing in *Churches of Old New England*, George F. Marlowe, an admirer of the classical proportions and tall steeples of Christopher Wren's London churches, saw early Puritan structures as "plain, boxy little meetinghouses, with a low and rather ugly belfry." Jenness described the Star Island meetinghouse tower: "Its elevated spire . . . a landmark for mariners; in dark and tempestuous nights, the warning light may have gleamed from its belfry; and in times of fog, the groping fisherman was guided safely home by the note of its friendly bell."

FIRST GOSPORT MEETINGHOUSE

To top their meetinghouse, Star Islanders sought the "Saints Bell" from the church on Smuttynose, by then collapsed and its timbers pilfered. The Saints Bell had been given to the old church by a sea captain or a pirate, and came into the hands of Roger Kelly. Kelly owned much of Smuttynose, where he had built his own personal fortune. Despite numerous convictions for selling liquor without a license, Kelly was variously constable, magistrate, and Shoals representative to Maine's General Assembly. Kelly refused to part with the bell, and Star Islanders took the case to the York County Court about 1700, charging "Mr. Roger Kelly . . . hath now this useless and silent Saints Bell in his secret Custody." Records of the outcome of the court case were lost, as was the Saints Bell.

The Eighteenth Century

The Shoalers "continued to maintain the meetinghouse" for the next fifteen years, but there was only an occasional preacher in its pulpit. Reverend Samuel Moody, son of Portsmouth's famous Reverend Joshua Moody, was pastor of the church at New Castle from 1694 to 1703. Moody never lived at the Shoals, but preached there from time to time. For a year, the governments of colonial Massachusetts and New Hampshire financially supported a minister at the Shoals. In 1705, the Massachusetts General Assembly granted fourteen pounds and the New Hampshire Assembly six pounds toward Reverend Daniel Greenleafe's support. Grants from the colonial legislatures were not renewed, and Reverend Greenleafe served just one year. Jenness wrote:

> When we consider that at this time there was a thriving community settled on Star, and that so considerable a contribution in those days as 20 pounds was requisite for the encouragement of the Congregational ministry there, it seems clear that the population felt quite indifferent to religious concerns.

The Reverend Joshua Moody (no relation to the earlier-cited Reverends Joshua and Samuel Moody) was the third of four Harvard-educated Congregationalist ministers of long tenure on the Shoals, but it is Betty Moody who is part of today's Star Island lore, rather than her clergyman husband. In 1724, during a threatened Indian raid that never happened, islanders gathered at the Star Island fort, but Betty Moody and her small children were on the other side of the island and hid in a cave—known ever after as Betty Moody's Cave. There she smothered her baby while attempting to suppress the infant's cry.

The Reverend Moody was never ordained, but, as phrased in *New Hampshire Churches*, "supplied from 1707 to 1732." Only an ordained minister could baptize, so from 1718 to 1726, the Reverend Theophilus Cotton, of Hampton Falls, baptized seventy-six Shoals children off-island or at the Shoals. Jenness cited a sermon by Reverend Moody that would have been typical of those preached two centuries ago to a congregation of fishermen—a story that has come down to us because of an unexpected response:

During the ministry of Mr. Moody at the Shoals, one of the fishing shallops, with all hands aboard, was lost in a North East storm in Ipswich Bay. Mr. Moody . . . addressed them in the following language adapted to their occupation and understanding. "Supposing, my brethren, that any of you should be taken short in the bay in a North East storm, your hearts trembling with fear, and nothing but death before you, whither would your thoughts turn? What would you do?" "What would I do?" replied one of these hardy sons of Neptune, "Why I should immediately hoist the foresail and scud away for Squam!"

Oscar Laighton also told this story in his *Ninety Years at the Isles of Shoals*, clarifying its punch line with an explanation of the geography of the area. "Squam [Annisquam near Ipswich] is a small harbor on the Massachusetts shore," he wrote, "south south west of Star Island, and dead to leeward in a northeaster."

Reverend Joshua Moody was at the Shoals when the first meetinghouse burned in 1720. Immediately after the fire, Shoalers built Star Island's second meetinghouse, also of wood. Shoalers petitioned the New Hampshire governor and General Assembly in 1721, pleading, "The charge and expense which they are at in the support of the ministry is as great as the people can bear at the present, it having cost them but lately the sum of Two Hundred pounds for that end in building a Meeting House—which is not yet all paid." Star Islanders' rapid replacement of their meetinghouse at substantial expense was in marked contrast to their lack of support for religion a few years earlier, and reflected their pride in Gosport's new status as a town.

The Gosport Church
and the Reverend John Tucke

In colonial New England, every town was required to "maintain religious worship" of the standing order, build a meetinghouse and provide a house for a clergyman, and support the minister through taxation of all townsmen. In time, that provision was somewhat modified so that taxes paid by a church member of another denomination went to his church rather than to the standing-order church. It was not until well after the Revolutionary War that churches came to be supported by the voluntary contributions of church members, primarily through pew rentals, rather than through taxes paid by all citizens of a town. The Isles of Shoals was not a town, however, nor was there a town on any of the Shoals islands until the New Hampshire General Assembly set apart Star Island in 1715 as the "Town of Gosport," annexed to Rye on the mainland for elections and assessments.

The town records of Gosport, reprinted in the *New England Historical & Genealogical Register* of 1913 and 1914, included a description of the formation of the Gosport church. Gosport leaders seeking "Settlement of a Minister among them" contacted "an Association at Portsmouth" that sent Reverend Nathaniel Morril of Rye. Morril "came over & the People readily agreed to have a Church Gather'd amongst them." Five men and eighteen women signed the Covenant of the Church of Gosport in June 1729.

Gosport's "gathered church" of just five men and eighteen women in the larger parish of Gosport was representative of the era's ratio of church members to townspeople, as was the preponderance of women as church members. "The parish" consisted of all male voters of a town, and thus all residents, but only those individuals within a parish who had made a public profession of faith were "the church." Some New England churches retain "parish" as part of their name to this day—for example, First Parish in Portland Unitarian Universalist Church and First Parish Congregational Church (John Brock's church in Wakefield).

Mainland Puritans took a close interest in the new church at Gosport and urged the congregation to "call" John Tucke, a Harvard College graduate of the class of 1723. At a time when class rank at Harvard reflected social status rather than academic standing, Tucke was seventeenth in the list of forty-three graduates. The first entry in the town records was the December 11, 1731, notice that "inhabitants of Star Island duly Qualify'd to Vote" meet "Monday next at nine of the Clock in the Forenoon to give the Reverend Mr. John Tucke a Call to settlement among us in the work of the Ministry." Notably, the entire parish participated in the vote to call Mr. Tucke, not just church members.

Early town records were detailed and included the treasurer's transactions. There were small amounts "To the School" through the 1730s, and the last reference to education in 1740 was "Mr. Nickolas Powers Chosen Schoolmaster for Six Months Next Ensuing for forty pounds." The relatively generous level of support for the school probably continued through most of Tucke's tenure, and the Gosport citizenry must have been relatively well educated. Town records soon lapsed into a more abbreviated format, apparently including only those items required by New Hampshire's colonial administration—a record that after proper notice a town meeting was held, evidence that the town met its obligation to keep the meetinghouse in repair and "support preaching," and the list of duly elected town officers.

Annually, the town of Gosport elected a moderator, three selectmen, and a treasurer, a constable, and a town clerk—probably the officers mandated for all New Hampshire towns. Gosporters also elected two "tythingmen" responsible for collecting each property owner's share of the town's support of its minister (later, a "quintal of merchantable fish"), a "wood corder" who gathered and distributed the driftwood that was islanders' fuel supply, and two "cullers of fish" who ensured the high standards of Shoals dunfish.

Negotiations between the town of Gosport and Mr. Tucke were recorded: a salary of 110 pounds and fifty pounds "toward building him a house," along with "a Convenient piece of Land for to set his House & a Garden Spot where he chooses if to be had" and "the Privilege of keeping one Cow." Tucke "declined a call to Chester in order to go to the Shoals." Reverend John Tucke's forty-one-year ministry to the Shoalers began in 1732 with his ordination in the Gosport meetinghouse and an apt ordination sermon from the biblical text Matthew 4:19: "You will be a fisher of men."

The townsmen increased Tucke's salary by thirty pounds in 1747, and three years later voted that his salary could be "paid in merchantable codfish" and that "every able man must help carry minister's firewood from the stages [dock] where it was brought from the mainland." Shoalers soon raised Tucke's salary to "a quintal of merchantable winter fish per man." Jenness explained, "As there were about one hundred men at that time on the Islands, and a quintal of fish was reckoned at a golden guinea, the salary was one of the highest at that time paid in New England."

Reverend Tucke was a behind-the-scenes figure in Gosport's town affairs, but he allowed his name to be first on a 1766 petition to New Hampshire officials to establish a lottery to build "a pier or basin at Gosport;" petitioners included many non-Shoalers with "names of great weight in the province." A bill to this effect was passed and "assented to by the Governor" in 1767, but the project "having proved impracticable, was shortly after abandoned." In time, private and federal funds built breakwaters enclosing the "Gosport roads," but there would be no substantial pier at Star Island until more than a century later.

"The Records of the Church of Gosport" was separate from the town records, and reprinted in part in the 1912 *New England Historical & Genealogical Register* as "Church Membership, Marriages, and Baptisms on the Isles of Shoals in the Eighteenth Century." Church records listed hundreds of infant baptisms, a departure from early Puritan practice of baptizing only infants of church members. All Gosport townspeople, whether or not they were church members, came to church to be married and to have their babies baptized, although neither infant baptism nor marriage was a church sacrament. Early Reformation leaders cut the seven church sacraments to two; adult baptism marked conversion with admission into church membership, and Eucharist commemorated Christ's Last Supper. There was no list of deaths in the church records; islanders must have followed an early New England practice of holding burials without clergy involvement.

Gosport baptismal records included both children and grandchildren of Reverend Tucke and his wife. John and Mary Tucke had eleven babies, but only Mary, Love, and John Tucke lived to maturity. Bithiah Tucke's baptism in 1736 was marked "This Child was Baptiz'd in Private," as were a few others—probably meaning a child who died at birth. Tucke also baptized "Candace, a Negro Child belonging to Mr. John Tucke," and in 1762 "Dinah, a daughter of Candace." Tucke's probated estate included the same "Diana, a Negro girl of about 12 years" valued at twenty pounds. Household slaves were common among New England clergy, more usually called servants.

The church records ended at Tucke's death, but occasional listings of nineteenth century marriages and births were entered by a family member in the town records well after the fact, usually as a list of all children of the marriage and their dates of birth. Less than half of the "Records of the Church of Gosport" were published in the *Register*—the complete manuscript copy has considerable additional information of interest to a historian of religion at the Isles of Shoals. Along with "Church Membership, Baptisms and Marriages," church records included the Confession (the congregational statement of belief) and the Covenant, as well as records of the Lord's Table, meetings of the Church Council, and the council's church governance and discipline.

Although the church records were in Reverend Tucke's handwriting, Reverend Morril, minister at Rye, prepared the Confession and the Covenant at the time of the formation of the church, three years before Tucke's arrival in Gosport. Morril's Confession and the record of Tucke's forty-one-year ministry should be read in the context of the era's First Great Awakening, the revival that swept much of New England for twenty years from 1725, with the Reverend Jonathan Edwards (second only to Benjamin Franklin as the most remembered name of that time) in a leadership role. Revivalists—the "New Lights"—preached the realities of hell, the sinfulness and unworthiness of their listeners, and the sweetness of repentance and salvation through Christ. Some "Old Lights" still preached the strict Calvinist view that God alone decides each person's eternal fate. That theology had been modified by many Old Lights, however, to what Edwards's biographer called "a broader, more tolerant, more reasonable religion" with a role for person's free will in choosing or rejecting salvation—a view that was moving toward the liberal and anti-Calvinist Arminians.

The Confession began with the basic Reformation tenet, "We believe God's Word or ye Holy Scripture to be . . . the only ground of our Faith." A just and compassionate God was once "Rewarder of those who diligently seek him [with] perfect obedience [to] the Moral law contained in the Ten Commandments," but because man "forfeited this happiness and incurred a contrary misery," only "Repentance and Grace through Christ . . . and a profession of Faith" sealed with "Baptism and the Lord's Supper" allowed a righteous person to be "judged to Life Eternal."

Significantly, the Gosport church statement of belief was not one of a predestined eternal life for a select few and inevitable damnation for the many, but rather an assurance that Gosport's church would "prepare adequately" its righteous members "for what is to be enjoyed in Heaven above." Morril and Tucke's theology that God grants forgiveness and eternal life to all who repent and believe places them among the Arminianists of the time.

The Covenant followed, with signatures of its twenty-two members and Reverend Morril's signed statement that "after a day of fasting and prayer," the members met at Mr. Joshua Moody's lodging "and signed the Covenant." The requirement for "full profession of heartfelt belief" and a public examination for convincing evidence of a "conversion experience" that was central to the first generations of Puritans in American had been tempered so that Shoalers were received into church membership with a simple prescribed affirmation of belief.

At a later meeting, "the Pastor and the Church" agreed "that the charge of the Lord's Table be carried on by a contribution of six pence apiece each time" (the only direct charge to church members) and that "the Sacrament of the Lord's Supper be administered the first Sabbath following the last Wednesday of each month." Reverend Tucke kept a careful record of the date of each Lord's Table, consecutively numbered from the "First Sacrament Administered on July 30, 1732" through number 365 on July 18, 1773, with the biblical text for each Lord's Table sermon. Like the first Lord's Table, the dates occasionally varied "by reason of some of the brethren's long absence from home by going to sea the next week." All church members participated in the monthly communion service, not just those judged "genuinely converted" as was the case with early Puritans.

Church records included the Reverend Tucke's occasional announcement of "a day of prayer and fasting," but the circumstances leading to these calls were not specified. Care for the destitute was both a town and a church responsibility, but town records did not mention charitable acts and only a single act of charity was recorded in the church records. Tucke wrote in 1753, "Upon my mentioning something of the great outward straits of a widow and member of the church," the church voted eight pounds "to be given to her," which Tucke delivered the next day.

In a remnant of the church courts that dated from the early Reformation, the Gosport pastor and its two deacons were charged with "exercising the government and discipline of Christ," defined in Tucke's time as keeping the Ten Commandments. Church records included Tucke's listing of "Confessions" (here meaning acknowledgment of wrongdoing)—and each confessor's appearance before the congregation was followed by "restoration to our communion." Beginning with a couple's "Public Confession of their breach of the Seventh Commandment," seven couples, three men and thirty-five women so confessed during Tucke's tenure. The ten men and forty-two women were roughly proportional to the twenty-three men and seventy women listed as joining the Gosport church in its church records.

There were other transgressions. In 1733, "The Church agreed that whereas our brother has been lately drinking to excess, he be put by from partaking tomorrow of the Sacrament and that he make acknowledgment of his sin by or upon the Sacrament next following for his restoration to our communion." In 1746, the church council heard a man's confession of "having been often guilty of taking the name of the Lord in vain, and of contention and quarreling," and a woman's acknowledgment "in shameful fashion [of] profane words . . . and sinfully absented herself from the sacrament in August." There was a 1746 problem of "bad carryings on with firing of guns," a 1755 confession of "acting and speaking very wickedly and sinfully defaming some of her neighbors" and another of one who "had wronged a neighbor," a 1756 confession of "repeating the sin of drinking," and a 1771 confession of "disorderly walking."

Tucke's Gosport church was not that of a fire-and-brimstone religion, and except for singling out an individual for a public confession of sin, it was a theology that a later Congregationalist would find appropriate. Only the transgressions of church members that could be deemed as breaking the Ten Commandments were subject to church discipline, and relatively few of Gosport's men were church members. Still, considering the half-dozen or so instances of public confession of wrongdoing other than "breach of the Seventh Commandment," Gosport was a veritable peaceable kingdom in the days of Reverend Tucke. Jenness paid tribute to Tucke:

> During the pastorate of Mr. Tucke, the islanders certainly exhibited more of the thrift and sobriety than they had ever shown before. His influence over them seems to have been strong and salutary. He was a man who attended to the material interests of his parishioners, as well as their spiritual welfare. He spent less effort in expounding abstruse dogmas they could not comprehend, than in inculcating morality and charity in the affairs of everyday life.

A town meeting early in 1774 discussed the "choice of Mr. Jeremiah Shaw to preach among us." Shaw accepted, but he was sick during much of his short tenure, although he lived to serve as minister of another church for thirty-five years. *The History of Rockingham County* noted, "From that time to the close of the eighteenth century the ministrations of religion at the islands were suspended."

A town records entry in 1775 (the last until 1799) made note of payment to Henry Andres "for hoisting the flag," and later events suggest this was a British flag rather than the flag of colonial New Hampshire, possibly reflecting the islanders lingering animosity toward anything out of Massachusetts, considered to be the center of the colonists' revolt. Soon after, even before the start of the Revolutionary War, New Hampshire ordered Shoalers off the islands so they could not aid the enemy; apparently, the islanders had neither claimed allegiance to New Hampshire nor declared their neutrality.

The transcriber's footnote to the 1799 town records entry explained that Massachusetts was able to clear all residents off Hog Island, and "New Hampshire endeavored to clear Star Island in the same way, but without success." On the eve of the Revolutionary War, there were 284 individuals at the Shoals, with all but about forty-four actually leaving for the mainland. Many of Star Island's buildings were floated to the mainland, and Tucke's son-in-law took his parsonage to York.

Dudley A. Tyng, of Newburyport, found the Reverend John Tucke's grave on his visit to the islands in 1799. In *The Isles of Shoals of Lore and Legend*, Rutledge quoted Tyng's journal entry of October 29, 1800: "Having accidentally discovered the Rev. Mr. Tucke's grave, I caused a decent Monument of stone laid in Mortar to be erected over it and intend to send a Top Stone with a suitable inscription." Tyng replaced the grave's modest marker with a horizontal slab of freestone, and composed the long inscription for Tucke's gravestone—possibly to remind Shoalers of a time when a man of religion walked among them:

> Underneath are the remains of the Rev. John Tucke, A.M. He graduated at Harvard College A.D. 1723, was ordained here July 26, 1732, and died Aug. 12, 1773, aged 72. He was affable and polite in manners; amiable in disposition; of great piety and integrity; given to hospitality; well learned in history and geography, as well as general science; and a useful physician, both to the bodies and souls of his people.

More than a century later, Edward Tuck, a kinsman of the Reverend John Tucke, who lived in Paris as an agent for an international banking company, financed construction of the Tucke Monument at Star Island. Edward Tuck also funded construction of the New Hampshire Historical Society's marble building, endowed the Amos Tuck School of Business

Administration at Dartmouth College, was a benefactor of the New Hampshire towns of Exeter and Hampton, and contributed five thousand dollars to the then new Star Island Corporation toward the purchase of Star Island.

Built in 1914, the Tucke Monument is a granite obelisk forty-six feet high on the Reverend John Tucke's grave, now within a circle of Star Island land owned by the New Hampshire Historical Society. Each of the monument's fifteen-ton granite blocks was transported from the dock on a wagon fitted with railroad wheels and pulled by a six-horse team over specially laid temporary track. Notably, Tucke Monument's inscription was copied from Tyng's horizontal tablet.

The Tucke Monument was dedicated on July 29, 1914, and commemorated in the New Hampshire Historical Society pamphlet "Dedication of a Memorial to Reverend John Tucke 1702–1773." After services at the memorial site, 238 guests dined at the Oceanic Hotel, followed by "adjournment to the convention hall" (now Elliott Hall in the Oceanic) to hear papers on Reverend Tucke and Captain John Smith. Two speakers evoked stereotypes of "ignorant fishermen" and "wild and turbulent members of his little parish." The third, however, cited Reverend Jedidiah Morse's sympathetic assessment: "Few parishes in New England at this period gave a more generous support to their minister, and few congregations were more constant and exemplary in their attendance."

Boston's Society for Propagating the Gospel

In 1787, a Boston group formed The Society for Propagating the Gospel Among the Indians and Others in North America. The society's work was to be supported by revenue from investments, and the society's original funds came from "a collection in all the churches of the state . . . by no means as productive as might have been expected" and a private subscription among society members and other "benevolent and pious persons."

Providentially, the society became the beneficiary of a bequest from "the late Hon. John Alford, Esq. of Charlestown," who died in 1761. Alford's will left "a large sum of money to be devoted to the purpose of spreading the knowledge of the gospel among heathen." Richard Carey, the executor of Alford's will, was elected to membership in the society soon after its incorporation, bringing with him access to the funds of Alford's estate. The society's first report noted, "His [Alford's] executor . . . had never, till the incorporation of this society, found any body of men to whom he might entrust this fund, with a prospect of its being applied agreeable to the intentions of the donor."

The society's first public report, the 1798 "Brief Account," was signed by the Massachusetts governor and state judges, signifying approval of the group's mission by authorities in high places, and for a few years from 1803, the Massachusetts General Court granted $500 to the society annually. Congregational clergy from churches in Boston and its surrounding area also signed the document, including Reverend Jedidiah Morse. Morse was probably the group's prime mover, and it may have been Morse who brought Carey and the Alford estate into the society. Jedidiah Morse was well known at the time as author of geographies and histories which later would go into many editions, and Morse was an expert on Indian tribes. Now it is his son who is better known—Samuel F. B. Morse was the inventor of the telegraph.

The society's "Brief Account" described its support for three missionaries to Indians in eastern New England, noting insufficient funds to send missionaries "into distant parts of the continent." Converting Native Americans to Christianity was a powerful notion for Americans through many years, taking the form of contributions to the missionary efforts of churches and missionary societies, and, for some, leaving a bequest at death for that work. In its first ten years, the society reported funding schools for Indians and distributing to them "38 bibles, 84 testaments, 150 spelling-books, 85 primers, 48 Watts' psalms and hymns, 18 Psalters, and 79 other books." The society also distributed "school books and books of piety and devotion among the poor inhabitants of the eastern parts of this common-wealth."

The society would soon turn its attention to the remote and isolated Shoalers. Three quarters of a century later, the Reverend William Leonard Gage, minister of the North Church of Portsmouth, was a frequent summer visitor to Gosport. Writing in *Summers at the Isles of Shoals,* Gage spoke of "rough and degraded islanders," with this tongue-in-cheek comment, "But they were not forgotten by the Christian World . . . When the Indians became scarce, it seems to have been taken for granted that the people next to them in point of savagery were the inhabitants of the Isles of Shoals."

Colonial Predecessors to the Boston Society

Although to our generation "Propagation of the Gospel" is a quaint phrase, it has historic roots, dating back to a Roman Catholic group of 1622, the Congregation for the Propagation of the Faith. Later, two similarly named English groups and a Scottish group figured in American colonial history. The London-based Company for Propagation of Gospel in New England supported work in the colonies among local native populations inaugurated by John Eliot, "Apostle to the Indians." Working through its commissioners of Indian affairs in Boston, the company published Eliot's translation of the Bible into an Algonquian dialect. The company also published the Bay Psalm Book in Boston in 1640–the first book written in the colonies and the first one printed in New England. As the Revolutionary War drew near, the group ceased activities in the United States, but continues to this day in Canada as the New England Company, supporting ministries among indigenous peoples.

An Anglican group, the Society for Propagating the Gospel Among Indians and Others in North America, was the best known of the colonial mission groups. It was organized in England in 1701, explicitly to promote the Anglican cause abroad—and implicitly to reinforce the reach of the British Empire and authority of the Crown. The society sent priests and teachers to boost the church's ministry to the colonists in America and to take the gospel to slaves and Native Americans. In this spirit, Queen Anne sent silver communion services to various tribes of the Iroquois Indians. Although the similarly named London and Boston societies were both referred to as SPG, the initials usually meant the Anglican group. By the Revolutionary War, three hundred SPG missionaries had served in the British colonies that would become the United States.

With American independence, SPG turned its attention to what became the British Empire, soon sending missionaries to the West Indies and Nova Scotia and later to India and South Africa. Over time, SPG's emphasis changed from funding churches serving Anglicans abroad to work among a country's indigenous peoples. After World War II, SPC was one of a number of Anglican mission groups that were merged into the United Society for the Propagation of the Gospel—still active worldwide, and partially supported by special collections in Anglican churches.

A Scottish group, the Society in Scotland for Propagating Christian Knowledge, sent missionaries to Native Americans, starting in 1730. It was this group that approached "a number of gentlemen in Boston and its vicinity" in 1762, asking if they could "superintend the funds of the society which were devoted to Christianize the aboriginal natives of America." As reported in the Boston society's 1798 "Brief Account," the archbishop of Canterbury "was jealous lest this should interfere with the Society established in Great Britain," and the king did not authorize a Boston group. But fifteen years later, as noted, a successor group to the "gentlemen in Boston and its vicinity" founded the Society for Propagating the Gospel Among Indians and Others in North America.

The Star Island
Stone Meetinghouse

A few Shoalers returned to the islands after the Revolutionary War and a few had never left. Star Island histories describe lawless years after the war, when the second meetinghouse was "maliciously burned." In one version, "the meetinghouse was wantonly set on fire about 1790 by a party of drunken fishermen, who held a wild revel by its light while it was burning." Similarly, Celia Thaxter wrote, "They burned the meetinghouse, and gave themselves up to quarrelling, profanity, and drunkenness, till they became almost barbarians." A less prejudicial account cited an overheated stove as the source of the fire, while Oscar Laighton explained the fire as islanders cutting up pieces of the wooden meetinghouse "to keep the pot boiling when they were short of firewood."

According to the *History of Newburyport*, Shoals fishermen applied for licenses to Dudley A. Tyng, port collector at the Customs House in Newburyport, on the coast of the Massachusetts mainland and within sight of Star Island; the office of port collector included responsibility for Newburyport's nearby islands. The Constitutional Convention of 1787 created a federal government with the power to raise revenue that, under the Articles of Confederation, had been a prerogative of the states. With citizen resistance to taxation, the federal government formed the Customs Service to collect duties on imports—for a time ninety percent of the new government's income. Soon after, in 1792, the newly empowered Congress of the United States passed the Cod Fisheries Act, providing for a bounty to cod fishermen to encourage fishing and trade and as compensation for the import duties on the salt essential to New England fishermen. A license from a customs officer must have been a prerequisite to eligibility for the cod bounty.

Tyng granted licenses to the Shoals fishermen, but "urged them to abstain from the immoderate use of spirituous liquors and curb their evil appetites." Tyng, a prominent Newburyport church layman with ties to Boston gentry, wrote to the Boston society on April 27, 1799 asking for help: "I am convinced that they are as wretched a little community as ever excited the Charity of Man . . . From what I learn, many of the Inhabitants are

grieved at this State of Things . . . They encourage the Idea that if some
person of a character suited to their wants could be induced to fix himself
among them, considerable portion of his support might be obtained from
the inhabitants."

The Boston society sent a missionary in 1799, and Tyng was elected to
the Boston society in 1800. The Gosport Town Records "in the hand of Rev.
J. Morse" reported events that Tyng set in motion:

> 1799 Sept—The Reverend Jacob Emerson of Reading (Mass) visited
> the Isles of Shoals, by desire & at the expense of "the Society for prop-
> agating the Gospel among the Indians and others of North America,"
> established at Boston, and spent three Months on the Isles, preached
> thirteen Sabbaths & taught a small school. The Society was induced
> to send Mr. Emerson to these Islands by a letter communicated to
> them from Dudley A. Tyng Esq. of Newburyport, describing in a
> most affecting manner the destitute & wretched situation of the
> inhabitants as to religious & moral instruction.

> 1800 Aug 6—The Rev Jedidiah Morse of Charlestown near Boston
> arrived at the Isles of Shoals. He was sent . . . to enquire into the state
> of the people of these isles as to the expediency of sending a
> Missionary or Schoolmaster to that place. He was furnished by the
> Society & other benevolent persons with the following books to be
> distributed among the inhabitants . . . Mr. Morse spent five days on
> the Islands, preached four times to the inhabitants, catechized their
> children, & distributed the books committed to his care. He found on
> Smutty Nose Island three families . . . with 20 souls. On Star Island
> alias Gosport he found 15 families containing in all 92 souls, the most
> of them in a state of great poverty and wretchedness such as to force
> the tear of commiseration, & draw from the human heart every effort
> to afford relief.

> 1800 Aug 10—About the year 1790, some of the people of the baser
> sort, not having the fear of God before their eyes, pulled down and
> burnt the meeting-house, which was a neat and convenient building,
> and had been greatly useful, not only as a place for religious worship,
> but as a landmark for seamen approaching this part of the coast. The
> special judgments of Heaven seem to have followed this piece of
> wickedness to those immediately concerned in it, who seem since to
> have given up to work all manner of wickedness with greediness. By

means of the exertions and benevolence of the Society for Propagating the Gospel, established in Boston, and some liberal minded gentlemen in Newburyport, Portsmouth and other places, there is a prospect and hope that another place of worship will be erected on the site of the old one, and the means of religious and moral instruction be again regularly afforded to the unfortunate and almost forsaken people of this islands.

In August and September 1800, Morse and Tyng visited the large churches of the seaport towns to raise money for a new church at Gosport. It was a time of maritime prosperity in New England—after the Revolutionary War and before the War of 1812—and Morse and Tyng were remarkably successful. Rutledge's Isles of Shoals histories of 1949 and 1971 drew from Tyng's report to the Boston Society: "Five hundred was subscribed in Salem, three hundred in Portsmouth, about one hundred in Exeter, and the remainder, about five hundred dollars, was taken up in Boston and Newburyport."

Equally remarkable, a meetinghouse of stone was built in a few days in October 1800. Stones had already been quarried and dressed and site preparation completed when on October 20 Tyng returned to Star Island with fourteen carpenters and materials. Rutledge cited Tyng's report to the Society: "On Wednesday the 29th we all returned to Newburyport having completed the Meetinghouse and repaired several Dwelling houses inhabited by the poorest of the people. I distributed some articles of Clothing and Bedding amongst them and some wood. About three cords of wood I stored for the use of the school this winter." Morse wrote in the town records:

1800 Oct. 29—This day the stone building on the hill is completed and it is intended by the donors to be used as a place of public worship and as a schoolhouse and it is hoped it may be useful as a landmark for seamen. The pews belong by purchase to the following persons, the minister for the time being, Mrs. Sarah Mace, Mr. John Caswell, Mr. William Pierce, Mr. Samuel Haley, Jr., and Mr. John Newton.

The Reverend Jedidiah Morse dedicated the meetinghouse on November 14, 1800, with his text based on Psalm 118:25, "Oh Lord, I beseech thee, send now prosperity." Morse later described the chapel as "an edifice of stone with a cupola . . . on the highest spot on Star Island, which answers the treble purpose of a place of worship, a school house, and a land-mark for seaman." Just as two earlier Star Island meetinghouses served to warn sailors away from the rocky isles, the new meetinghouse had a tower as a beacon to seamen, along with a belfry with a bell to sound on foggy nights—predating by twenty years the federal government's Shoals lighthouse on White Island.

Morse also noted, "The Society for Propagating the Gospel and several booksellers in Boston gave books and stationery suited to their circumstances, sufficient, with proper usage, to last several years." Jenness wrote, "Morse interested himself deeply and efficiently in procuring these benevolences, and also in providing for the spiritual and temporal welfare of the Shoals people for many years after." Parents of an island baby born soon afterward named their son Jedidiah Morse Haley.

Morse, ever the geographer and perhaps with his own entrepreneurial aspirations, prepared a formal report on the Isles of Shoals that was published in the Collections of the Massachusetts Historical Society in 1800. His report was divided into sections titled "Harbor," "Face of the Islands," "Climate" (Morse, like others, found summer "delightfully cool and salubrious"), "Productions," "Water," "Population" ("four or five families excepted, [these are] a miserable set of beings, extremely poor, dirty, and wicked"), "Present State of the Islands," "Fisheries," and "Eighteenth Century Conditions." Morse's enigmatic concluding paragraph was at odds with his notation that Gosport's chapel of stone and, by inference, its community of religious people "will be imperishable:"

> Should Massachusetts and New Hampshire cede their right to these islands to the United States (a plan which some have contemplated), and the federal government should think it expedient to establish them as a free port, and form a harbor, and erect the necessary fortifications and lights, they would soon become a place of much importance to the United States.

The Boston society sent the Reverend Josiah Stevens to the Shoals in 1801, paying him $300 a year. Tyng likely arranged the appointment—Stevens lived in Newburyport, where he helped found one of its churches and was a deacon. Stevens had "served two short terms in the Revolutionary War . . . and a fellow-soldier spake of him, as a man of decided piety, who amidst the bustle of camp, was constant in his morning and evening devotions."

At Gosport, according to *The History of Newburyport*, Stevens "was for several years the officiating clergyman, preaching to a good-sized congregation on Sunday, and during the remainder of the week teaching the children how to read and write." Stevens, then widowed, boarded with the Samuel Haley family on Smuttynose, and married the Haleys' daughter Susanna— the bride was 45 and the groom was 61. As noted in the town records entry of May 27, 1801, "This day Mr. Josiah Stevens, Missionary at this place, was married to Miss Susanna Haley of the Isles of Shoals." The Newburyport history continued, "By the exertions of Mr. Tyng, money enough was raised . . . to build and furnish a parsonage house on the very spot where the house of Mr. Tucke had stood."

Town meeting records up to 1804 were signed "Josiah Stevens, Justice of the Peace." Without commenting on the incongruity of a man of the cloth serving as a town's law enforcement office, Jenness wrote:

> Mr. Stevens received a commission from the State of New Hampshire, as a Justice of the Peace; and appears to have acted with vigor in his office. In one of his letters to Mr. Tyng, he asks for a pair of 'stocks,' and from a subsequent communication to the same gentleman, we learn that he received and used, with good effect, those now anti-quated instruments of punishment for evildoers. But he was removed in the midst of his usefulness by death.

Reverend Stevens died in 1804, and his wife soon afterward. Stevens and his wife were buried on Star Island near Reverend Tucke's grave; the minis-ter's name was spelled Stevens in the records, but Stephens on his gravestone. The engraving on the recumbent gravestone can still be read: "In memory of Reverend Josiah Stephens, a faithful instructor of youth, and a pious minis-ter of Jesus Christ (Supported on this Island by the Society for Propagating the Gospel)."

Newburyport's Society for Promoting Religious Instruction

Jenness said of Morse, "By his recommendation, the Society for Propagating the Gospel continued to send out missionaries for many years to the Islands." In actuality, though, there was no settled minister at the Shoals for the twenty years after Reverend Stevens's death, and none funded by the Boston society for thirty years. Rutledge's list titled "Isles of Shoals Ministers, Missionaries, Teachers, and Agents" identified those who were Boston society appointees, and included a number of men at the Shoals over the thirty years after 1804. Except for Reverend Samuel Sewall who served two years, however, each was on the islands only briefly.

For a time, a second group took interest in the Shoalers. As described in *New Hampshire Churches,* "In 1822, a society of gentlemen, with a ladies' auxiliary society, was formed in Newburyport, for the religious instruction of the people of the Isles of Shoals, which supplied a teacher for about nine years." Newburyport's Society for Propagating Religious Instruction at the Isles of Shoals raised money in Newburyport, Salem, and Boston. Unlike the larger missionary societies of broader scope, the Newburyport group was founded to serve the narrow and specific purpose of religious instruction at the Shoals, and it was a teaching mission rather than a preaching one. Four Newburyport ministers representing a Congregational church and three Presbyterian churches were signatories to the society's reports.

In a town records entry initialed M.A.D., "Mary A. Davis came to this Island from Newburyport by the request of Mrs. Jane Greenleaf of that Town, Treasurer of the Society for promoting religious instruction among the People residing on the Isle of Shoals. Kept a school on Star Island one year." The Newburyport society then sent "the excellent Miss Peabody" to teach and, in Celia Thaxter's words, to "reclaim the little children from wretchedness and ignorance."

The Third Report of the Newburyport society (1824) said, "The progress of the scholars in learning has been as great as was reasonable to expect . . . Seven of the poorer female children were taken to lodge at the parsonage . . . to preserve them, as much as possible, from the influence of an evil example, which they were almost continually compelled to witness in their parents." Miss Peabody wrote, "There has been, in some degree, an increasing sobriety. Some of the children, particularly, who had begun to tread the paths of intemperance, have been checked and redeemed."

Miss Hannah Peabody soon had her lodgers "carding and spinning when out of school," and her schoolchildren produced 138 yards of cloth, 356 skeins of yarn, and 100 yards of fishnets "from materials provided by the society." The cloth was made into garments for schoolchildren and given to the poor of the islands. Writing in the late 1860s, Celia Thaxter said, "I saw in one of the houses, not long ago, a sampler blackened by age, but carefully preserved in a frame; and was told that the dead grandmother of the family had made it when a little girl, under Miss Peabody's supervision."

Miss Peabody also ran a Sabbath school, and "often read to several of the people . . . such religious discourses as were thought to do them good." According to the 1823 report, several islanders asked, "if, in addition to Miss Peabody's labors, we [the Newburyport society] would keep a Missionary with them six months of the present year, they would, themselves, furnish something toward his support." In 1824, the Newburyport society was able to send "Mr. J. Ely as a permanent teacher, wages $200.00, and the Reverend Samuel Sewall as minister at $300.00." A town records entry said, "Rev. Samuel Sewall departed this life in Rye March 16, 1826, where he went on business, after seven days sickness with a Lung Fever."

The interior of the stone meetinghouse burned in 1826. According to Louise Tallman's "Some of the Families of Gosport at the Isles of Shoals," soon after the fire, Reverend Sewall left the island in ill health to return to his family home. On his way he "visited Portsmouth and other places to obtain funds for rebuilding his meeting-house on the Isles of Shoals, which had been burnt down." Jenness quoted from Tyng's journal, "The interior wood-work was partially destroyed by fire on January 2, 1826, but shortly after was restored by the bounty of religiously disposed people of the mainland, and dedicated anew in 1830." Tyng's "shortly after" was, in fact, four years.

The Seventh Report of the Newburyport society (1829) noted, 'The number of inhabitants increased over two years, from 70 to 90," concluding, "Even the small number of 90 preparing for an eternal existence ought to be favored with knowing in what manner that existence may become one of happiness." *New Hampshire Churches* reported, "After the death of Reverend Mr. Sewall, the regular preaching of the gospel, by Congregational ministers, was suspended."

Gosport town records entries resumed with the note, "The Society at Newburyport for Promoting Religious Instruction at the Isles of Shoals visited this Island in September, 1830, and dedicated the New Meeting House."

1832 May 25—The Society then invited Clementina B. Pierce of Portsmouth to instruct the School on Star Island, under their patronage . . . She accepted their invitation, and instructed the school for 9 months. The school consisted of about 30 scholars, between the ages of 2 & 15 . . . The most of them were bright, intelligent children; their improvement was good, generally speaking.

The next town record entries related to young men who came to the Shoals from the Theological Seminary at Andover "at the solicitation of some benevolent individuals of Newburyport." Three students spent a weekend conducting a revival, and soon after, a student spent five months at Gosport.

1834 Aug 18—Our efforts commenced on Friday night, at the house of Mr. Joseph Caswell with prayers and exhortations. On Saturday P.M. a meeting was held in the meetinghouse and the people were addressed by Mr. Cleland and Mr. Muzzy from Rev. 3:20. A meeting was held on the evening of the same day when Mr. Cleland addressed an attentive audience from 2 Cor. 5:20. In the morning of Saturday we with some friends from Newburyport visited the school of Mrs. Chickering [formerly, Miss Pierce and by then a visitor], with which we were highly pleased. Sabbath morning we visited the Sabbath School. At 10 o'clock Mr. Pratt preached from Prov. 1:24-27. At one in the P.M. Mr. Pratt again preached from Hebs. 2:3. The people paid good attention. In the evening Mr. Muzzy preached from Luke 19:42. The house was fuller than at any previous time during our visit.

1835—Being employed by benevolent individuals residing in Newburyport Robert W. Fuller came to this Island, Nov. 7, 1834, for the purpose of instructing the young people and laboring for the spiritual benefit of the whole population. He remained on the Island about five months, during which time he taught a school, addressed the people from the word of eternal truth three times on each Sabbath when the weather would permit, and held other religious meetings, and delivered two addresses on the subject of Temperance.

The Newburyport society became inactive, but Newburyport's support of the Shoals mission continued through the efforts of Miss Jane Greenleaf, who died in 1851. Miss Greenleaf wrote that she had "one object . . . the spiritual improvement of the people living on the Isles of Shoals." Her memoirs were quoted in *New Hampshire Churches.*

> For the last thirty years of her life, she cordially cooperated with those who sustained a mission there (the Shoals); and after she had entered her seventieth year, the principal care of providing ministers and teachers and of raising funds for their support, was voluntarily assumed by herself, until her growing infirmities obliged her to relinquish it. She often received a few dollars for "the Shoals" as a providential favor. These people were constantly remembered in her prayers; and much did she rejoice, when any report of their improvement reached her ears.

Thomas Laighton and the Appledore House

In 1839, Thomas Laighton bought four of the nine islands at the Isles of Shoals in 1839 with plans to revive the Shoals fishing industry—Hog (now Appledore), Smuttynose, Malaga and Cedar. Samuel Haley had acquired Smuttynose Island about 1770, known as Haley's Island for many years.

Haley and his family were able to raise grain and "coax cherry trees into abundant fruitfulness," and built a major commercial center at Smuttynose, with windmills to grind grain and wheat; a brewery and a distillery; saltworks, "which manufactured excellent salt for the curing of fish;" a ropewalk; a dock; and the Mid-Ocean House of Entertainment. The Haleys became the most prosperous family at the Shoals, and gained title to Hog Island properties deserted by owners in their move to Star Island. Thomas Laighton's acquisition of the islands once owned by the Haleys prepared the way for the Star Island Corporation's purchase of Appledore Island in almost its entirety ninety years later.

Laighton obtained an appointment as keeper of the White Island light in 1839 as a way to be closer to his developing Shoals fishing business which would soon employ ten men and send "hundreds of barrels of mackerel to Boston." Laighton brought his family—his wife Eliza, four-year-old Celia, and baby Oscar, with Cedric born a year later. The Laightons' years at the lighthouse have been memorialized in the writings of both Celia and Oscar, and romanticized in children's books. Celia wrote of the Laighton children in *Among the Isles of Shoals*, "I do not think a happier triad ever existed than we were, living in that profound isolation."

HALEY HOUSE

Earlier generations of the Laighton family had been prominent in Portsmouth business, and Thomas Laighton owned wharves and ships with his brothers. He had been a postal clerk, customs collector, and newspaper editor, and was active in politics, serving in the New Hampshire Senate. Laighton was well known, and even at White Island lighthouse, eminent New Englanders visited the Laightons. After two years, Laighton was elected to the New Hampshire House of Representatives.

The family lived at Smuttynose in 1841 and 1842 while Laighton served in the House, and Thomas Laighton enlarged Samuel Haley's Mid-Ocean House of Entertainment. The Laightons entertained summer visitors at the Mid-Ocean House for seven years. Levi Lincoln Thaxter, a Harvard College and Law School graduate, was an early summer visitor, and Laighton later engaged Thaxter to tutor his children, who, until that time, had been taught by their father.

Laighton began planning for development of the Shoals as a summer resort. His Portsmouth business was successful, his fishing business was profitable, and by 1847 he had sold his share of the family holdings in Portsmouth for capital. In a short-lived partnership with Levi Thaxter, Laighton borrowed additional money from Thaxter's father to build a large luxury hotel on Hog Island, which he had renamed Appledore Island. The Appledore House opened in 1848 with accommodations for 130 guests.

Celia Laighton was sixteen when she married twenty-seven-year-old Levi Lincoln Thaxter at Appledore House in 1851, and their first son was born a year later. Nathaniel Hawthorne visited the young couple during his two weeks at Appledore House in September 1852. Hawthorne's diary speaks of spending evenings drinking apple toddies with the Thaxters in their cottage. On his last evening there, Hawthorne and the Thaxters enjoyed a glass of fine old wine—at a time when missionaries in the Gosport pulpit were preaching against the evils of drink.

Thaxter had taken an interest in the village at Gosport, and attended a service in the Gosport meetinghouse on one of his first trips to the Shoals— the town records of 1852 included the entry, "L. L. Thaxter Esq. visited the school March 4th and expressed his gratification & pleasure to observe the good attention & attainments of the scholars." Later, Thaxter gave "18 spellers and six arithmetics" for the Gosport school. The Boston society engaged Thaxter in 1853 as Gosport's schoolteacher and interim lay minister. This was an unusual appointment, probably made in view of Thaxter's Boston connections and the Thaxter family wealth. At the same time, the

Boston society appointed Reverend John Mason, but Mason did not come to the Shoals until September 1854. Until then, Celia and Levi Thaxter lived in the parsonage; they vacated it and left Gosport on Mason's arrival.

Curiously, Celia Thaxter never mentioned her year in the Star Island parsonage in *Among the Isles of Shoals*, although she wrote of Reverend Mason, the second missionary, as "an excellent man." Much later, though, Oscar Laighton wrote, "My sister always said that those were the happiest days of her married life." Sarah Orne Jewett's preface to *The Poems of Celia Thaxter* recalled Jewett's visit with Celia Thaxter near the end of her life and "a long afternoon among the high cliffs of Star Island where we sat in the shade behind the old church, and she spoke of the year that she spent in the Gosport parsonage, and went there with us, to find old memories waiting to surprise her in the worn doorways, and ghosts and fancies of her youth tenanting all the ancient rooms."

The tone of the memoirs of Celia Thaxter and Oscar Laighton suggests that the simple people of Gosport were a world apart from the Laightons. In his foreword to the facsimile reprint of *Among the Isles of Shoals*, Frederick T. McGill said of the Shoalers that Celia was "among them but not of them." In Portsmouth, Thomas Laighton belonged to the Universalist church, and his wife's family were prominent Episcopalians, and Celia Laighton's youth at the Isles of Shoals coincided with the years of the activities of the Boston and Newburyport Societies at the Shoals, but her writings did not mention attending church services at Star Island. In *Among the Isles of Shoals*, Celia Thaxter wrote reverentially of early preachers at the Shoals, "these were good and faithful men," but pejoratively of the missionaries, "'divine service,' so called, has seemed a mere burlesque as it has been often carried on in the little church at Star."

Thaxter severed his relationship with the Shoals soon after his missionary service, although he did not give up his financial interest until 1870. He had a near-death experience sailing in a skiff from Portsmouth to Appledore Island in 1855. Thaxter and Celia were growing apart, and neither showed any further interest in the chapel serving the fishermen of Star Island. Celia Thaxter spent winters on the mainland and summers with her family at Appledore Island, raising her children, helping her invalid mother, welcoming Appledore House guests, and writing poetry. Celia Thaxter's first published poem, "Landlocked," appeared in the *Atlantic Monthly* in 1861, and her first book, *Poems*, came out ten years later. *Among the Isles of Shoals* was published serially in the *Atlantic Monthly*, and then in 1873 as a book.

The Appledore House flourished, and Oscar Laighton wrote of this period, "Starting in 1848, we were the pioneers in establishing a summer hotel on the New England Coast. A dozen years later there were several along the shore, from Rye Reach to the islands off Portland Harbor. In 1860, Appledore House would accommodate three hundred people, and more rooms were needed."

Shoalers in the
Early Nineteenth Century

Celia Thaxter said of the Shoals fishermen, "They lead a life of the greatest hardship and exposure, during the winter especially, setting their trawls fifteen or twenty miles to the eastward of the islands . . . It is desperately hard work, trawling at this season, with the bitter wind blowing in their teeth, and the flying spray freezing upon everything it touches—boats, masts, sails, decks, clothes completely cased with ice."

Fishing was dangerous; even today, its occupational fatality rate in America is second only to that of timber cutting. Although later replaced to some extent by wages, fishing's traditional compensation system of "sharing the catch" pushed fishermen to desperate risks. Each man "fished on his own hook," bringing his own equipment, food, and bedding on board, and profits were divided by established fractions among the owner, captain, and crewmen. Each crewman had something to gain when fishing was successful and a large catch sold. When a boat docked with an empty hold, however, all went home with empty pockets.

Public houses were commonplace in preindustrial England, and came with Englishmen to the New World, where they were central to the public life of each village. There had been a tavern at Smuttynose from the earliest times, probably serving "bounce" (spruce beer mixed with wine) with Madeira for the more prosperous clientele, as well as "several ale houses" on Hog Island. Significantly, the Reverend John Brock did not record a problem with alcohol among the Shoalers. By 1700, though, ever-increasing trade with the West Indies brought rum to the taverns of the British colonies in America.

With rum as the prevalent drink, liquor abuse did become a problem. Celia Thaxter wrote, "Those who lived here centuries ago were decent, God-fearing folk," but the islanders "fell into evil ways, and drank 'fire-water,' and came to grief." Jenness said of the Shoals:

The shifting, heterogeneous characters of the population [was not] conducive to sobriety or stability . . . Taverns and ale houses abounded on all the Islands, and we may be sure their walls echoed with the hoarse company, as they quaffed their tankards of beer, their . . . Barbados strong waters, or "their liberal cups of rum-bullion."

As noted, Dudley A. Tyng chided Shoalers for "immoderate use of spirituous liquors" and appealed to the Boston society for a missionary to counter the influence of strong drink. The words of the society's Reverend Jedidiah Morse ever after characterized Shoalers as "drunken" and "degenerate." The temperance movement had an early start in New England, with a temperance society founded in Boston in 1826. Later, in 1851, Maine was the first state to pass prohibition legislation.

Later Missionaries
of the Boston Society

The Reverend Andrew P. Peabody was pastor of the South Parish in Portsmouth in the 1830s and 1840s, where, according to *New Hampshire Churches*, "A society of ladies there [Portsmouth] has been active and persevering in their efforts for this people, their benefactions being liberal, frequent and long continued." The teaching mission sponsored by citizens of Newburyport was followed by the Boston society's resumption of interest in the people at the Shoals, the addition of a teaching component to its religious mission, and the annual provision of $250 toward support of a missionary and a teacher at the Shoals.

Reverend Peabody was elected to the Boston society in 1840, and represented the society as supervisor of the Gosport Chapel until he left Portsmouth in 1853 for Boston. The society's 1843 report affirmed its "confidence on the intelligence, fidelity, and zeal" of Reverend Peabody "whose local position affords all needed opportunities of judgment." Portsmouth's South Parish "had been led into Unitarianism in 1819," and Reverend Peabody was a prominent Unitarian, but the clergy Peabody recruited to serve at the Shoals were neither Congregational nor Unitarian. His first recruit was the Reverend Origen Smith, a Free-Will Baptist.

With the Boston society's renewed work at the Shoals, its missionaries found much to deplore, and temperance became a major crusade. Jenness wrote, "In 1835 the Rev. Origen Smith went to live at Star, and remained perhaps ten years, doing much good among the people. He nearly succeeding in banishing the great demoralizer, liquor, and restored law and order. He is reverently remembered by the Islanders," then numbering about one hundred. Jenness cited Reverend Smith's 1840 report to the Boston Society:

> The cause of temperance is slowly advancing. About forty belong to the Temperance Society, which excludes intoxicating liquors. The person who sold spirits this past year has abandoned the sale, joined our Society, delivered an excellent address to the people, and pledged his future influence on the side of temperance. There is one man here

who keeps spirits to sell to strangers and water parties; but he does not sell to the inhabitants on the islands.

In 1843, the Reverend Smith was failing in health, and Mr. Ritson, "licensed to preach by the Christian Baptists," was in the Shoals pulpit. Mr. Ritson was not an ordained minister, so Reverend Peabody procured Reverend Hall, "a Christian Baptist minister of approved character and standing." Reverend Hall's report to the Boston Society said, "Knowing that intemperance was the greatest curse that ever fell upon these people, I began with my might to put the tyrant down." In contrast to Hall's assessment of himself as a powerful orator, Richard Henry Dana Jr. of *Two Years Before the Mast* fame and an early summer visitor to the Isles of Shoals in an 1843 diary entry pronounced Hall an ineffectual speaker:

> Walked to church at ten in a violent rain and gale. Congregation of about 25 persons . . . The sermon was from the text, "Thou shalt not take the name of the Lord thy God in vain." Flat, wandering and miserably weak was the performance . . . Once he alluded to his own want of education and said that there were some present who could tell better than he could such and such things. This was pitiable, and only served to lower him in the estimation of his people. I doubt if he can do much good among these people, for although it is not necessary that their clergyman should be learned, yet they are shrewd and need a man of more force and common sense.

In 1844, the society reported that Reverend Peabody secured Reverend Abraham Plumer, "a preacher of the Methodist persuasion" and "a man eminently successful in waste places and on stony ground." Taking note of Thomas Laighton's Mid-Ocean House of Entertainment on Smuttynose Island, Dana had written in his diary, "It is said that the Laightons mean to sell spirits. If they do there will be a fierce contest, for either they or the Islanders will be broken up about it."

But Plumer's letter in the Boston society's 1846 report was encouraging: "Our Temperance Society is doing well; although we had a death-like influence cast around us, by the establishing of a rum-shop upon one of these islands, by the man who attends the light-house here." A year later, Plumer again extolled his progress in the temperance area. Taking note of the beginnings of the Shoals as a destination for summer visitors, he wrote, "We have just passed through the season when we are flooded with company from the main land, and many of them of the baser sort."

Coinciding with Abraham Plumer's arrival, Gosport's town records were resumed, with an 1844 entry noting that no "annual or legal meeting of said Town has been held since 1804." Plumer soon became integral to the affairs of Gosport, keeping town meeting records and serving as town meeting moderator and Gosport representative in the New Hampshire Legislature. Oscar Laighton remembered hearing of Reverend Plumer as "a most worthy man," and recalled an old story: "If a school of mackerel came into the cove at meeting time, the congregation would rush out of the meeting house for their boats, with Elder Plumer not far in the rear."

Mr. Plumer's claims of success and his leadership role in the town notwithstanding, the Boston society's 1848 report intimated trouble— "Circumstances had arisen . . . awakening the inquiries of the Committee." The secretary of the society visited the island and found "the aspect of the church spoke ill for the love of neatness and order or reverence in the people; it bearing in nothing the appearance of a building that had been swept or garnished for many months." Expediently, Plumer had left the Shoals just before the secretary's visit, but despite the 1848 report's intimation of a severe reproof, Plumer was "authorized to spend a few months" as the society's missionary at Mantinicus Island off the Maine coast.

The society also sent teachers to the Shoals—Miss Mary A. Davis in 1843 and 1844 (the same Mary Davis who taught Shoalers under the auspices of the Newburyport society in 1842), Miss Cordelia Frisbe in 1846, and Miss Nancy J. Underhill in 1847 and 1848. Of Miss Davis, the society "believed that the pupils could not be entrusted to a more intelligent or faithful care." Miss Frisbe reported that she was "encouraged to labor for the dear youth here, for they have minds susceptible of improvement."

In the Society's 1847 report, Miss Underhill wrote that she was teaching her thirty-four pupils "geography, grammar, writing, reading and spelling. Nearly all the girls connected with the school devote a portion of every day to needlework . . . This school will not suffer in comparison with any of the same age with which I am acquainted . . . Many of the youth in this place are ready to bless your Society . . . for the means of a common school education." The society's secretary who found the Shoals church in disarray on his August visit wrote approvingly of the school—"One redeeming feature we gladly notice, which was that presented by the day-school of Miss Underhill, its late skilful and faithful instructress." The society's 1848 report told Miss Underhill's tragic story:

In precisely a month from this day of visiting her school, Miss Underhill, accompanying some friends to a favorite spot, where she was accustomed to spend many of her leisure hours in witnessing from the rocks God's glories in the deep, was suddenly overwhelmed by a rising wave, and withdrawn at once and for ever from the scenes of earth.

Miss Underhill's body washed ashore on the mainland a week later. Ever since, the Star Island rock where she had been sitting has been known as "Miss Underhill's Chair." Downs explained, "This chair was reasonably above water when the tide was average or low but when the waves were riding in high it was a dangerous spot for they would wash right up over the rocks." However, the town records' transcriber took issue with the "washed from the chair" story:

The accident occurred near the so-called 'Chair,' but she was not washed from the Chair itself. She was out with others to watch the very heavy surf. The popular tale that others have been washed from the Chair appears to have only this foundation, that in 1864 Eveline Caswell of Gosport and Lydia Varrel of Rye together were washed off the rocks, but below this place and nearer to Southern Point.

While the Boston society funded partial support of a missionary and a teacher at Gosport, the town was responsible for maintenance of the meetinghouse and parsonage. An 1845 town meeting agenda item had been "to raise and appropriate such sums of money as is found necessary to defray the expense of the town for support of the school," and the town "voted to raise nine dollars school money." Two years later, the town had voted "$15 to be raised for the school." The town's minimal funding contributed to the poor condition of the school and meetinghouse.

The Boston society's termination of Reverend Plumer's appointment, in effect, was a censure of Reverend Peabody's supervision of its Shoals mission. The town fathers recognized the importance of continued support from the society, particularly for a teacher, and hastened to make amends through a unanimous town meeting resolution of March 12, 1849:

Whereas the Society for Propagating the Gospel has benevolently assisted us in the means for moral and mental improvement for many years & whereas the Rev. A. P. Peabody of Portsmouth has been an active agent in thus doing us good, therefore

Resolved 1. That we hereby express to Rev. A. P. Peabody and through him to that Society & others our sensibility of their benevolence and our grateful acknowledgements for their labor of love, and

Resolved 2. That although we may not always have appreciated as we ought to have done their acts of kindness, we will hereafter if our privileges may be continued Set a high value upon and make a better improvement of them.

The town also recognized that its own miserliness was at fault, and "voted to expend the Surplus Revenue for the best good of the town," including "$125 to repair the meeting house and school house should it require so much." The transcriber noted, "The Surplus Revenue here devoted to public purposes appears to be the money obtained for the town by the Rev. Abraham Plumer when he served as the representative of Gosport in 1848." After Plumer's departure, an entry in the town records by the town clerk paid tribute to him, and in contrast to the society's words of disapproval, reflected the townspeople's appreciation of Reverend Plumer's activities on their behalf:

During his stay among us, the Schoolhouse was built, the Parsonage house repaired and chimney built and porch also annexed to the back of the house. The barn was also built . . . He collected what he could but did not obtain sufficient to defray the expense. He did most of the work himself. He was a member of the State Legislature from this place and obtained from the Treasury a surplus revenue which we did not receive at the time it was divided to other places."

Mr. Blodgett, Plumer's replacement at the Shoals, told the society, "The number in attendance at church on the Sabbath has been gradually and constantly increasing. Men who had not been to church for years, as I am told, have for a few Sabbaths past been there. The last Sabbath our congregation numbered sixty-four, and for the last four weeks have averaged fifty. This, we think is doing well, considering that but few attend from the other islands, though I have visited them all, and that it must be remembered there are but eighty inhabitants on this island." The Town Clerk's note in the town records presented a markedly different picture, however: "His [Plumer's] successor to the Ministry was the Rev. L. D. Blodgett from Rye, N.H. who continued among us up to Sept. 29, 1849, when it became manifest to his employers that for lack of interest in his labors he could accomplish no good among the people, and he was permitted to leave."

After the Boston society's displeasure with both Plumer and Blodgett, the society "actually withdrew its aid for a time," according to the town record's transcriber. Persuaded by the town's 1849 resolution of appreciation to the Boston society and "some other petitions, together with the intercession of Mr. Peabody," the society reconsidered, and sent Oliver D. Eastman "both as the Missionary to the people and Teacher of their School." A town record entry dated "1851 and 1852" said of Eastman, "Came to commence his labors June 13th and generally had three meetings on the Sabbath when his health and the weather would permit, and some evening meetings during the week. Had a Sabbath-school regularly of about twenty children." Reverend Eastman was the subject of Hawthorne's 1852 diary:

> "By and by I had a glimpse of the good man himself in his suit of black, which looked in very decent condition at the distance at which I viewed it. His clerical air was quite distinguishable, and it was rather curious to see it, when everybody else wore red-baize shirts and fishing boots, and looked of the scaly genus."

In March 1851, before the Reverend Eastman's appointment, the town "voted against the sale of spirituous liquors in the Town." Although Gosport was in New Hampshire, this was coincident with Maine's prohibition law—a law not correspondingly honored at Laighton's Appledore House in Maine. Reverend Eastman seems to have given attention to issues other than temperance. He had a flair for public relations, and secured a number of gifts for the Gosport school and mission: a library of books from the American Sabbath School Union, a set of maps from some individuals in Newburyport, a bell "weighing ten pounds" (later exchanged for books for the library), a large Webster's dictionary, and "a quantity of tracts."

The Reverend Eastman garnered good will for the society and its mission by bringing influential visitors to the Gosport school. According to in the town records: "During the winter some more interest was manifested in the subject of Religion. Some were reclaimed from a backsliding state and expressed their resolution to serve the Lord the remainder of their life . . . The school was visited by Rev. Mr. Peabody and Mr. Foster with some others from Portsmouth, also Gov. S. Dinsmoor of Keene, N.H. and several other gentlemen who expressed their gratification in finding our school in so prosperous a condition."

As noted, the Boston society appointed Levi Lincoln Thaxter as lay preacher and schoolmaster in 1853, and in 1854 the Reverend John Mason came to Gosport as an ordained minister. Reverend Mason led a singing school, probably teaching hymns in three-part harmony—Celia Thaxter called it "a most excellent institution." At that time, Shoalers must have still been singing the "metrical Psalter" that arose out of early Reformation opposition to the lavishness of Catholic Church music; Psalms were sung without accompaniment to a tune of the leader's choosing. Celia Thaxter's recalled an earlier Shoaler, "long since gone to another world . . . He used to be head singer at the church, and 'pitched the tune' by whistling when the parson read the hymn. Then all who could joined in the singing."

Jenness quoted Mason's 1855 report to the society, "In the relations they sustain to the missionary, they require of him more than is just and proper. He must have the whole care of the public buildings. This includes repairing, cleansing and preserving from injury . . . Unconscious of any impropriety, they have sought the missionary to mow their grass, file their saws, repair their clocks, pull their teeth and make coffins for the dead." Like the reports of most of the Boston society missionaries, Mason's final words had the same justification of project cost and the necessity for its continuance as a present-day nonprofit group's report to its funding agency:

> In conclusion, I would add that withdrawal of those humane Christlike influences, which your Society has through so long a period, exerted on this population . . . would be ruinous. Their degeneracy into a kind of civilized heathenism would be rapid, and the Shoals would soon show one of the most desolate, hopeless moral wastes in New England.

A town records entry in 1857 noted, "The Rev. George R. Beebe Minister of the Gospel . . . with a wife and two children, came here April 1856. He is also Doctor among us, and is liked both as a Preacher and a Doctor. The inhabitants of Gosport have given him about eighty dollars in presents and money the year past." Beebe almost immediately became town clerk, and his early town records included items of general town interest.

About 2000 visitors during the season of 1858.

A U.S. Surveying Steamer enlivened our harbor by her prolonged presence and her soundings were evidently made with care and completeness.

Some of our young men tried to better their circumstances by engaging elsewhere in fishing, but finally concluded that they could do about as well at home and so returned.

In consequence of an improvement in fishing tackle a great many more fish are now taken in winter than formerly.

Nearly all the families in the place either take or have access to a weekly newspaper.

The soil of the islands is gradually lessening, which fact suggests that future generations will yet be compelled to bury their dead in the sea or secure burial on the mainland.

Several Missionaries here have broken down under the labors of the Day School and the Pastorate. In this very bleak situation, especially in winter, and subject to the irritation to the lungs which incessant breathing of salt air induces, it is no wonder that their lungs and vocal organs fail them.

Like his predecessor, Reverend Eastman, Beebe marshaled support for the Gosport church and school from the outside world. Well aware of the need to assure the Boston society that its mission was important and contributions essential, Beebe wrote in the town records in 1858:

Conscious of the value of Education, Pastoral Care, and Medical Assistance, the people now, more than formerly, Contribute liberally toward Securing them. But in consequence of the Smallness of their number and limited means, they are still dependent on the assistance of the Society for Propagating the Gospel and other friends in Portsmouth for the principal amount required to sustain these interests.

According to the *History of Newburyport*, "The Gosport chapel has been kept in good order and condition by the occasional contributions of visitors who attend divine service on the island during the hot summer months." One of Beebe's entries in the town records noted, "Several Gentlemen visiting the Shoals and friendly to the mission enterprise here, Charitably Contributed toward its sustenance." Oliver Shaw of Utica, New York, in 1858 "presented our Sabbath School with a very acceptable library containing 100 volumes," he wrote. Beebe likely hinted to Shaw that participants in Reverend Mason's singing school five years earlier were ready for organ accompaniment, and in 1859 Oliver Shaw "presented the Missionary with a beautiful melodeon, to be used in the church. Its sweet notes are a treat to many and an attraction for others to attend service."

The islanders gave a weather vane for the meetinghouse—appropriately in the shape of a codfish. The town records of 1859 noted, "At a considerable expense, the inhabitants of these Isles have put up a beautiful vane on our chapel. May their own hearts yield to the breathings of the Divine Spirit, as that vane does to the winds." "Renewed" in 1947 and regilded in 1977, the codfish still tops the chapel tower.

In 1859, Reverend Daniel Austin, of Portsmouth, presented a bell for the Star Island meetinghouse. That bell rang for 45 years, until it ceased during the 1924 General Conference. A 1924 conferee wrote, "The bell did not ring the Call to Worship, and announcement was made that it was broken. Two days later, again it was heard, one of the men having climbed up in the Belfry, and struck the rim the required number of times, thus enabling it to continue its work."

Beebe also worked with Reverend Austin to fund and build the Captain John Smith monument in 1864. Beebe may have prodded the Boston society to purchase the parsonage; it had been built in 1802 with funds raised by Dudley Tyng that were not funneled through the Boston society. The *History of Newburyport* noted that the dwelling house was erected "for the use of the minister or missionary residing on the Isles of Shoals forever," and it must have been considered as belonging to the town of Gosport. The transfer of parsonage ownership from the town to the Boston society removed the expense of parsonage maintenance from the islanders.

Like another of his predecessors, Reverend Abraham Plumer, Beebe took a leading role in the town's management and its affairs. Writing in 1875, Reverend Gage chronicled Beebe's roles at the Shoals: "minister, doctor, surgeon, dentist, lawyer, justice of the peace, teacher (also the school committee), representative in the New Hampshire Legislature, collector of revenue for Gosport, inspector of customs, United States Commissioner, selectman, general letter writer, police chief, apothecary, and father of a family." Gage's list has been frequently cited, and Beebe himself extolled his value to the citizens of Gosport in describing his routine activities in his annual report to the society, reprinted by Frederick McGill in *Letters to Celia*:

Retires at ten o'clock, rises at six . . . About fifty nights in the year this rest is broken by calls of the sick, made upon him in his medical capacity. Breakfast at eight, the two hours previous, after rising, being spent in private devotion, reading the Greek Testament and other biblical studies, after breakfast, family devotions. At nine o'clock the round of the sick is made, there being commonly from three to twenty on his list as physician; then reading and study and dinner occupy the time till two o'clock p.m., and the remainder of the afternoon is devoted to pastoral visits: the missionary aiming to have direct religion conversation with everyone over seven years of age at least once a month.

A town records entry in March 1859 voices Shoalers' support for the Abolitionist cause on the eve of the Civil War: "As usual [the town meeting vote of 1859], the Democracy prevailed in the contest for State and county officers. By this however is not to be inferred that the Democrats here are in favor of Slavery. No. There is not a man on the Shoals, of whatever party, but would help to free the suffering slave of the south and be glad to see him a self-reliant, intelligent and God-honoring fellow creature." There is a note of righteousness in Beebe's town records entry in 1859, suggesting town officers had long evaded proper practices. At this meeting, he wrote, "a disposition was generally manifested to do town business legally. Especially was this the case in regard to taxation."

In 1862, Beebe entered the tax lists in the town records for the first time. Thirty persons were listed, including one woman; all but eight owned land or buildings, and the property of two of the others was just "a cow." There was no similar tax list in the 1863 records, and the March 1863 town meeting, in the words of the records transcriber, "may not have been held legally," so "certain legal voters of Gosport" petitioned that a second meeting be held. Their interest seemed to have been in challenging the tax list.

An undated entry in the town records that may have been from late in 1862 said, "According to Act for the Enrollment of the Militia, the following persons constitute the militia force of this town." Thirty men, from the age of nineteen to forty were listed and the age of each given, with a disability noted for six of the men. An announcement for a March1863 town meeting listed as agenda items "To see what sums the town will raise for the men who shall be drafted in this town and to take action under the Statutes of this State in reference thereto as the town shall think best" and "To see how much money the town will raise for the support of the families of the men who shall be drafted from this town." The town's need for revenue to meet the town's Civil War-related expenditures markedly increased taxes.

Although there is no record of a subsequent meeting, the transcriber found a page with "an extended plan for a tax list . . . but only a few entries are made, and these are confused by many figures and calculations written in at random." The transcriber reproduced the entry for Downs' grandfather J. B. Downs that listed his homestead valued at $824, "brining field" at $224, flake ground at $300, $70 in money, $20 in stock in trade, two cows worth $35, and one dog (no value), a total of $1,475, compared with Downs's 1862 value of $960. It may have been an across-the-board increase in assessments and a corresponding 50 percent increase in taxes that led townspeople to contest the 1863 tax list. Shoalers' commitment to the abolition of slavery wavered when it came to financial support.

Sadly, the Beebes had lost three daughters to diphtheria in 1863. Mitty was off-island at school in Kittery, where she caught the disease. It spread to two of her sisters, and Mitty, Jessie, and Nellie Beebe, then eleven, seven and four, respectively, died within a month of each other, in May and June. The three little girls were buried in the Beebe Cemetery near the future site of the Captain John Smith monument. Reverend Beebe had earlier built a family cemetery, apparently intending to stay at Star Island. He found a hollow with earth in a remote section of the granite island and surrounded it with a wall of cut rocks topped with an iron railing. The railing is gone and the site overgrown, but the Beebe family's marble monument remains, along with small headstones for Mitty, Jessie, and Nellie.

Beebe's entries as town clerk ended in 1862, and there was nothing further in the town records about the Civil War, but an 1865 *Portsmouth Chronicle* article reported Beebe's war service and his return to the Shoals:

We are glad to see that the Rev. George Beebe, M.D. has returned alive and well from the brilliant campaign resulting in the capture of Richmond, during which he served as a surgeon. His old parishioners at the Shoals have made a strong effort to induce his return among them, subscribing toward his support more than twice as much as ever before, and almost unanimously petitioning the Venerable Society for Propagating the Gospel (hitherto mainly supporting the Mission at the Shoals) to send him there again as their minister, teacher and physician. In their petition they express, as the result of nine years' experience, the utmost confidence in the pastor and his wife whose united influence has ever been strongly in favor of moral and social improvement and the Christian life.

Reverend Beebe retired from his Shoals ministry in 1867, but continued to live at the Shoals for a time. Beebe was the missionary of longest tenure, serving thirteen years to 1869. Downs's memoirs attest to Beebe's good work. Downs's father "secured the main part of his education in the little school house and church" during Beebe's tenure, and was given a Bible in 1865 when he was nine years old "because he was able to read it all the way through." Downs's mother "went to the school on the Island and was reared in the Advent religion. The pastor and teacher at the time was the Reverend Beebe, whom she admired for his never-ending work on the Island. She, also, in later life, became a Baptist Advent in Portsmouth."

The last missionaries at the Shoals served brief terms. Reverend Gage remembered calling on one of these men: "He was not in, but his wife received me and told me the story of their discouragement. Religion had touched the lowest point in the church, and the gospel got not even a hearing. 'True,' she said, 'there are plenty of sistern who come to meetin', but not a brethren ever comes.'"

From Downs's description of the last years of missionary work in Gosport in the 1860s, the missionaries can be said to have met with some success: "There were the free thinkers and the strictly religious," he wrote. "There were some who drank and some who would not touch a drop under the threat of death. There were the men who listened respectfully to the solicitous advice of the visiting missionaries, who frequently came over to save their souls from utter destruction, and men who inwardly withheld their own fixed ideas of what was right and what was wrong."

Town records ended before the resolution of the 1863 valuation dispute, but a number of unrelated family entries had been inserted on blank pages near the end of the book. In one, "Mr. Benjamin Downs Departed this life April 1854. Mrs. Abigail Downs Wife of the above Departed this life December 1856." The transcriber noted:

> This entry forms an interesting link between the final pages of the Gosport Records and the first. This Abigail Downs appears to be the granddaughter of that Peter Robinson and Agnes Down who were married by the Rev. John Tucke in 1733, during the very first year following his ordination at Gosport. With another Agnes, her twin sister, and as the daughter of John Robinson and Elizabeth Down, she shared the baptism of 15 Aug. 1773 . . . the last act of Tucke's long ministry on the Shoals . . . A couple of years later she became a widow, and then married Benjamin Downs. She and her second husband are

the "Nabbaye" and "Bennaye" of Celia Thaxter's sketches, in which she is praised as an industrious woman and a good housekeeper when well along in years and lacking physical attractions.

The Isles of Shoals were essentially non-churched during the later Appledore House years, when Celia Thaxter greeted the famous and the artistic. According to *The History of Rockingham County*, "divine service has occasionally held in the old church on Sundays in summer by clergymen of various denominations passing a season at one or the other of the island hotels." A newspaper article pasted into the Town Records described a service at the Gosport church on the death of General Grant in 1885. Jenness published *The Isles of Shoals* in 1873, ending his section on ministers at the Shoals with these words, "For several years past, the pulpit has had no incumbent, and one by one the little band of parishioners has passed away from the islands." However, the demise of Gosport was not the gradual decline that Jenness inferred. Before Jenness' book was in print, the town of Gosport had come to an abrupt end.

Star Island
and the Oceanic Hotel

Oscar Laighton wrote of the early 1870s: "Appledore was famous for the distinguished visitors who came every year . . . and [it was] becoming the gathering place for literary people . . . We had raised our prices a little, as we were now running the hotel on modern lines, with the best chef and baker we could procure, and a gilt-edged head waiter. There were fifty girl waiters in the dining hall, with lace caps and full regalia."

Gosport villagers found work in the Laighton enterprises, and began to welcome summer people to Star Island. Laighton guests visited Gosport; Richard Henry Dana, Jr., for example, spent time there during a long stay at the Mid-Ocean House on Smuttynose, and later Nathanial Hawthorne at Appledore House took "passage for Star Island, in a boat that crosses daily whenever there are passengers." Gosport began to experience a bit of spillover prosperity from visitors looking for a good lunch and a guide. Downs's older brother "used to get paid for showing where Miss Underhill's chair was and for telling over and over her story." Downs and his sister would "go out on the beach and pick up shells from the rocks . . . string them together and sell them to hotel guests for fifty cents a string."

The Laighton's success invited emulation on Star Island. Joseph Caswell built his thirty-three-bed Atlantic House during the 1850s—"famous for its chowders, its fresh fish, and its doughnuts"—and summer visitors began coming to this and other small summer boardinghouses. By 1862, Joseph

ATLANTIC HOUSE

Caswell was the wealthiest man on the Gosport tax list. He died that year, he and his wife were buried with fine tombstones in the Caswell family cemetery, and Lemuel succeeded his father as proprietor of the Atlantic House. A fire at Gosport in 1866 burned the Atlantic House "with barn, bowling alleys and other outbuildings," and Samuel Caswell's Caswell House also burned. The town records book was kept in the Atlantic House, and the transcriber noted, "A few of these remaining pages are much besmoked and brittle, as though the book had been in a fire."

A third Caswell, Origen (named after the missionary Reverend Origen Smith), in 1867 built the Gosport House—a temperance hotel in which no alcohol was served. Lemuel Caswell soon rebuilt, and an 1868 *Portsmouth Evening Times* paragraph reads, "We understand that Mr. Samuel Caswell is about to erect a large hotel [the Caswell House] on the spot where the former building was burned. The Shoals is one of the most popular watering places in this section of the country, and its only drawback has been a want of accommodations."

Writing in the late 1860s, Celia Thaxter described the "tumble-down fish-houses and ancient cottages" of twenty years before, but reported that many of the buildings had since burned, implying that they had been set on fire by owners, "the object being to obtain the insurance thereupon." Since then, though, she wrote:

> There is not a vestige of those dilapidated buildings to be seen . . . and they have even cleaned out the cove, and removed the great accumulation of fish-bones . . . Many of them [the people of Gosport] show a growing ambition in fitting up their houses and making their families more comfortable . . . The old houses have been replaced by smart new buildings, painted white, with green blinds, and with modern improvements . . . and almost everything is white and square and new.

Appledore House was thriving when John Poor came to the Shoals. Oscar Laighton wrote, "One day in August of the year 1872 a man from Massachusetts, named John R. Poor, arrived at Appledore . . . Mr. Poor had been with us a few days when we discovered that he was secretly buying out the inhabitants of Star Island and the whole village of Gosport . . . Mr. Poor succeeded in getting possession of Star Island, and the people moved to the mainland." As reported in the *Portsmouth Evening Times*, "Business was done in the name of Mr. N. F. Mathes," but "Boston capitalists" were thought to be associated with the project. Once the transactions were completed, John Poor, of Boston's Stickney & Poor spice and mustard company family, became Star Island's sole owner.

At an 1872 town meeting, residents voted to deed all of Gosport's common lands to Poor's agent for a payment of thirty-eight hundred dollars to cover the townspeople's 1871 and 1872 taxes and the town's Civil War-related debts. In 1876, the New Hampshire Legislature approved annexation of the town of Gosport to Rye. Parsons wrote in his *History of Rye,* "The transfer was not asked by Rye nor by the inhabitants of Gosport; the transfer added but little to the valuation of Rye and nothing to its voting list of population."

John Poor owned the Star Island properties of all but two Gosport villagers, "having purchased nearly the whole island for between $53,000 and $54,000." The town records' transcriber noted, "It is well known that at this time there was much disagreement in the town affairs among the Gosportians . . . It is also pretty clear to those familiar with the conditions of these stormy times that the existence of jealousies and quarrels made the inhabitants ready to sell out when the chance came, despite the fact that the place was well on the way to prosperity."

Gosport families left Star Island for a new life and livelihood on the mainland, apparently with mixed emotions. Writing in 1873, Cedric Laighton told his sister, "Nearly all the Gosportians have been over here latterly, and they one and all say that they bitterly regret having sold their homesteads." John Bragg Downs and his wife remained, and were "last of the old-time Isles of Shoals people to retain and occupy a homestead on the Island." Oscar Laighton continued:

> In September a big gang of men were at work on Star Island, clearing away the old dwellings to make room for a large modern hotel. Mr. Poor seemed a man of matchless energy and unbounded capital, and before we had fairly recovered from our astonishment, his new hotel was being built . . . Work at Star Island was being rushed with a large gang of men all winter that the new Oceanic Hotel might be ready for the next summer . . . On the twentieth of June, in 1873, both hotels at the Isles of Shoals, with flying colors, swung wide their doors . . . We found the new hotel did not harm us. All our old guests stuck to us, and the tremendous advertising of the Oceanic was bringing new people to Appledore.

The Reverend Gage, however, wrote, "I always go to Star . . . partly because one of the best hotels in the United States stands upon it . . . the splendid and sumptuous Oceanic with all of its modern splendors"—including its elevator, said to be the first hotel elevator in America. After three seasons, the Oceanic Hotel burned to the ground, dramatically reported in the November 12, 1875 *Portsmouth Chronicle*:

> At about 2:30 o'clock Thursday morning a bright light awoke Portsmouth citizens, which proved to be at the Shoals, ten miles off . . . There were 147 sleeping rooms, capable of accommodating 300 guests . . . Probably little if anything was saved. The grand piano was nearly new and one of the finest to be had. The bake house and laundry had all the modern conveniences and improved machinery . . . There was $125,000 on building and furniture. Poor said his investments amount to about $325,000 . . . The island and original buildings as they now stand are probably valued as high as $90,000.
>
> During the seasons of '73 and '74, the business was conducted at a heavy loss on account of lack of patronage . . . [Poor funded an] addition of a wharf costing $30,000, blasted away ledges, macadamized a street, created a lawn, and removed old buildings. With the pleasure season there came a renewed patronage and at the time of the ocean yacht race the hotel was filled to overflowing. For the first time business paid interest on the investment, and taxes.

Poor's stone pier was the first substantial wharf at the Shoals, and still extant in today's dock, although extended, repaired, and rebuilt through the years. Oscar Laighton wrote, "Mr. Poor, with dauntless energy, commenced at once to build the present Oceanic Hotel before the ashes of the first building had cooled off. The new hotel, though not as large, had a finer view than the first one, and in many ways was more desirable." Laighton went on, repeating a phrase he used earlier: "It was rushed with a big gang of men during the spring and was ready for the opening in June."

Before the 1875 fire, Poor was planning an addition to his hotel; he had already purchased lumber for that purpose and stored the hotel's crockery and linen in the parsonage. Poor's new Oceanic Hotel incorporated the Caswell hostelries, with the Atlantic House as its east end, the Caswell House at the rear, and the Gosport House at its west end—names that continue to this day. The three boardinghouses were joined to a large new central structure built from the lumber intended for the addition and housing the grand lobby.

However, as Oscar Laighton wrote, "Mr. Poor was never a hotel man, and he was unfortunate in his managers . . . At the end of the summer of

1875, Mr. Poor came to us, offering to sell his holdings at Star Island for what the island alone had cost him." The Laighton brothers hesitated to accept Poor's offer. Thomas Laighton had died in 1866, and Cedric and Oscar Laighton were running the Appledore House. They expanded the hotel, necessitating a bank loan, but by the time Poor built his first hotel, the Laighton brothers' indebtedness to the bank "was being gradually wiped out." Oscar Laighton explained their dilemma:

> It was very tempting, but we were hardly in a condition to raise a hundred thousand dollars and mother and Cedric were not in favor of the purchase, but most of our friends thought we ought to secure the property, arguing that the Archipelago was unique . . . that there would always be a great summer business here . . . Everything looked so propitious, we bought the property.

A few years later, a fine veranda was constructed along the front of the Oceanic Hotel, extending across four large village houses moved to be in line with the Oceanic (Cottages A, B, C, and D). Oceanic brochures announced, "In connection with the hotel are a number of cottages, large and small, especially adapted to the needs of families. They are connected with the hotel by piazzas and electric bells, and have all the benefits of hotel service." In 1891 "terms" were "$3.50 per day; by the week, $21.00 a week; by the month, $17.50 a week." Importantly, "Mails arrive three times daily, and from the newsstand daily papers may always be obtained."

An early brochure boasted, "The Oceanic Hotel is one of the largest and most complete Summer Hotels on the New England Coast, noted for its sanitary excellence and unequalled location . . . The Hotel has a fine Billiard Room, a large Ball Room, Bowling Alley and Lawn Tennis Court, and a large fleet of fine boats for sailing or rowing, manned by experienced skippers in connection with the Hotel. An orchestra is always engaged for the season." Oceanic brochures always touted Shoals fishing opportunities: "The Cod Fish Banks are within a few minutes sail. The fish are abundant and of very large size. A prize is offered each season for the guest catching the largest cod. The heaviest cod landed any season thus far weighed 76 $^3/_4$ pounds."

The Laightons advertised widely, produced enticing brochures, and, in a publicity coup, had a fanciful description of a family day trip to the Isles of Shoals published in *The Bay State Monthly* in 1884, titled "Reuben Tracy's Vacation Trips." The fictional Reuben Tracy and his family boarded the steamer *Appledore* in Portsmouth, dined at the Oceanic, "a hotel kept by the same proprietors as the Appledore House," and then had time "to look around."

They visited the chapel "with about twenty-five pews," noted its weather vane "in the form of a fish, which crowned the little wooden tower," and "wished they had time to read some old preserved records of that place, which could now be seen at the hotel." The family saw the "horizontal slabs" marking graves of the Reverend Josiah Stevens and the Reverend John Tucke, and "some willows and wild roses, enclosed in a wooden fence" with the graves of "three little children of a missionary who once lived on the island." They read aloud the inscription on the large rock where "Miss Underhill, a loved missionary teacher, was sitting, when a great wave came and washed her away."

Oceanic Hotel brochures claimed, "Eminent physicians all over the country advise a sojourn here as productive of wonderful results," and announced that a physician was always on the premises. Dr. Joseph W. Warren, professor of physiology at Bryn Mawr College, was the Oceanic's physician from 1881 through at least 1912. The 1891 Oceanic brochure listed "the Town Records of Gosport" among the "many interesting historical relics of that quaint and peculiar town." Dr. Warren transcribed the handwritten Gosport church records and town records, printed in the *New England Historical & Genealogical Register* of 1912, 1913, and 1914.

Dr. Warren wrote, "For some years the book of town records remained as a curiosity for the edification of the summer visitor at the hotel on Star Island," and he originally read them there, but later the town records were taken to the New Hampshire Historical Society. The separate Gosport church records were removed from the island at the time of the Revolutionary War, and had since been in the hands of various clergymen. They were eventually donated to the New Hampshire Historical Society, where Dr. Warren transcribed the portion that was published in the *Register*. Dr. Warren's interest in Gosport history was also evident in his compilation and careful labeling of an early photographer's pictures of the village of Gosport, recently discovered and published along with an anthology of early writings as the 1997 book *Gosport Remembered: The Last Village at the Isles of Shoals*.

In the meantime, Celia Thaxter's writings, especially *Among the Isles of Shoals*, brought many to the islands, and the heyday of the Appledore House continued for some years. Oscar Laighton wrote, "Appledore Island was next to Concord, in Massachusetts, as a gathering-place for distinguished people," rating a long chapter in Frank Preston Stearns's 1895 *Sketches from Concord and Appledore*. Stearns wrote, "Mrs. Thaxter's poetry was the making of

Appledore as a summer resort. Between 1865 and 1875 thousands of people came every summer to catch a sight of her." Longtime guests bought lots from the Laightons, and built large "cottages" on Appledore.

Alan Emmet's essay on Celia Thaxter's garden in his 1996 book on historic New England gardens said, "Celia herself, her parlor, her garden, and the island became ever more wrapped in romance from the 1860s, when her first poem was published." Celia Thaxter's 1874 *Poems* was reissued in 1876, and she published another book of poems, *Drift-Weed,* in 1879. Celia Thaxter's parlor was a literary and artistic mecca, and Stearns wrote of the many "wits, geniuses, and brilliant women" gathered there. Childe Hassam became one of Celia's inner circle, and Hassam's painting of Celia's parlor, *The Room of Flowers,* became one of his best-known pieces of art. Hassam painted four hundred works at the Shoals, many featuring Celia's beloved Shirley poppies, which, in her words, "make the garden look as if the dawn had fallen into it out of the sky."

Celia Thaxter died at age fifty-nine in 1894, a few months after publication of her book *An Island Garden,* lavishly illustrated by Childe Hassam. She was buried in the Laighton family cemetery on Appledore Island, visited today by many. The Laighton cemetery is enclosed by low stone walls, and the tall marker on the graves of Thomas and Eliza Laighton lists their names on one side and the names of their children on the other. Smaller gravestones mark the resting places of Celia, Oscar, and Cedric. There is a gravestone in one corner for Celia's children, Karl, John, and Roland Thaxter, and a gravestone in another corner for Roland's three daughters (his young son was buried elsewhere). John's daughter, Rosamond Thaxter, was buried in Kittery Point; she wrote *Sandpiper,* the 1963 biography of Celia Thaxter.

Oscar Laighton matter-of-factly summarized changes in the Laighton family, the Shoals hotels, and his financial situation:

> After we lost our sister there was a change in the fortunes of Appledore. Her beautiful garden and the attraction of her parlor were greatly missed. Hundreds of summer hotels were springing up on the Maine and New Hampshire coasts, and the railroads to York Beach and Hampton were taking the transient business our steamer used to get. Our big hotels were barely paying their expenses. The insurance on the Appledore and Oceanic properties amounted to three thousand dollars a year; then the interest on our indebtedness to the bank called for four thousand more. It seemed impossible to stem the advancing storm. In 1899 my brother died. That was the greatest blow of all.

The Elliotts at the Shoals

During the declining years of the islands' hotels, Mr. and Mrs. Thomas Elliott came to the Shoals. A Children's Chapel at the All Star I conference in 1997 imagined the event.

Narrator: One hundred and one years ago Mr. Elliott was an important member of his Unitarian Church in Massachusetts. Each summer members of his church and other churches met for a conference. But in the summer of 1896, Mrs. Elliott was ill.

Mr. Elliott: I'm worried, my dear. You have been sick all spring, and it is time to pack for the Unitarian conference at the lake in New Hampshire where we meet our friends from other churches.

Mrs. Elliott: *Cough, cough.* Maybe I'll be better when I get there. But it is so hot at the lake. *Cough, cough.* I can hardly breathe. *Cough, cough.*

Mr. Elliott: Dearest, you haven't been getting better since being sick last winter. I have an idea. Instead of the hot lake, let us go where it will be cooler. The Isles of Shoals are ten miles out to sea. Let us go there.

Mrs. Elliott: *Cough, cough.* Where would we stay? How would we get there?

Mr. Elliott: There are two hotels. The Oceanic Hotel is on Star Island and the Appledore House is on Appledore Island. We will go on a steamship.

Mrs. Elliott: *Cough, cough.* Oh, that sounds cool and lovely. Do let us go!

Narrator: And so, instead of their church conference at the lake, the Elliotts took the steamship to Star Island and its Oceanic Hotel. Five days later:

Mrs. Elliott: This sea air is wonderful. I feel better and I'm not coughing anymore.

Mr. Elliott: You look much stronger, my dearest, and your cheeks are rosy again.

Mrs. Elliott: I so wish our Unitarian friends could be here with us. Wouldn't it be grand if they could come to the Shoals?

Mr. Elliott: What a good idea. Maybe we all can come here together next year.

Mrs. Elliott: How glorious that would be. We could have our summer conference here. We could hear sermons and sing hymns. We could talk with our friends on the porches. We could sit on the rocks and look at the ocean and the sky.

Mr. Elliott: I'll ask the hotel manager if we all can come next summer.

Narrator: So Mr. Elliott talked with Harry Marvin, who managed the Oceanic Hotel and Appledore House for Oscar and Cedric Leighton.

Mr. Elliott: We had such a good week. It would be heaven if our Unitarian friends could join us at the Shoals.

Mr. Marvin: Maybe your friends could come here next year.

Mr. Elliott: But $3.00 a day is too expensive.

Mr. Marvin: $3.00 a day is how much we charge. Lately business hasn't been very good, so maybe we could charge a little less. How much do you pay at the lake?

Mr. Elliott: We pay $10 for the week.

Mr. Marvin: How many people go to your conference? If lots of them came, maybe we could charge less.

Mr. Elliott: I could bring 500 people. Most would be Unitarians, and some would be from other religions.

Mr. Marvin: Then I will charge each person $10 for the week.

Mr. Elliott: Excellent, my good friend. I pledge to fill the Oceanic Hotel and Appledore House to the ridgepoles with the first Unitarian Summer Meeting at the Isles of Shoals.

Narrator: Mr. Elliott worked hard to get 500 persons to come to the Isles of Shoals in 1897, filling every room of both hotels. The summer conferences continue to this day, and Thomas Elliott returned to the Isles of Shoals each summer for 40 years.

Unitarians

The Shoals hotels were already the meeting site for some organizations; there is an 1886 group picture of the Boston Commandry in the Oceanic. Still, Oscar Laighton's record of his conversation with Harry Marvin expressed his concern about Thomas Elliott's plan to bring Unitarians to the hotels the following season: "I told him that we must act with caution. 'What is a Unitarian? Are they good people? It won't do to introduce any rough element.' Harry said that he did not know just exactly what a Unitarian was, but, judging from the Elliotts, he would say that they were very nice, harmless people."

Oscar Laighton's "What is a Unitarian?" sets the stage for a history of the denomination. New England's established church (the standing order) was Puritan, but one hundred years after the first Massachusetts Bay Colony, Puritans' church membership and influence had fallen off. Later generations of Puritans no longer had the same intensity of faith as their fathers.

About 1725, the First Great Awakening brought a wave of revivals to colonial churches in New England and elsewhere. Congregations were caught up in the emotionalism of revival services that emphasized human depravity, the graphic horrors of eternity in hell, and the essentialness of the conversion experience. Membership in evangelistic churches grew with the newly converted, and by the Revolutionary War, the name Congregational was coming into use to differentiate standing order churches from other New England religious groups. It was some time, though, before Congregationalism ceased to be the established church in New England and thus the one supported by taxation. "Disestablishment" came to New Hampshire with the Toleration Act of 1819, then to Connecticut, and finally, in 1833, to Massachusetts.

Even before the Revolutionary War, many in eastern Massachusetts were influenced by the rise of rationalism, and growing apart from the orthodoxy and harsh features of the standing order. After the Revolutionary War, evangelistic revivalism of the Second Great Awakening modified the stricter aspects of Calvinistic predestination and innate depravity to belief in the possibility of salvation through personal faith and devotional service. But differences between orthodox revivalists and liberals were unbridgeable, particularly in Boston. Conservative clergy preached against "the Boston Heresy," and conservative ministers refused to exchange pulpits with liberal clergy.

"The Unitarians effectively captured Harvard," with the appointment of Reverend Henry Ware, Sr. to the Hollis Professorship of Divinity at Harvard College, and soon the Divinity faculty was Unitarian. The Honorable John Alford's will that provided support for gospel propagation among Indians also endowed a Harvard chair, created during this period as the Alford Professorship of Natural Religion, Moral Philosophy, and Civil Polity. "Natural religion" comprised those doctrines the reasoning power of man could support.

Reverend Jedidiah Morse was in the forefront of conservatism. Morse preached against the liberalism of Harvard, and with dissident Harvard faculty, helped found the orthodox Andover Theological Seminary in 1809. Like English Puritans, and later, John Wesley's Methodists—who chose to remain nominally Anglican rather than separate from the Church of England—New England liberals had not intended to be a group outside the established church. Morse and other conservatives, in effect, forced liberals to leave the Congregational church.

Morse, in derision, used the term "American Unitarianism," even though rejection of the Trinity had not been a significant issue within liberal churches. The liberalism of eastern Massachusetts had grown out of the tenor of the times as well as from new understanding of the New Testament through consideration of its historical context—not the anti-trinitarianism of English Unitarianism. William Ellery Channing responded to Morse, endorsing the new identity with his "Unitarian Christianity" sermon in 1819. Channing said the truth lies not in "the irrational and unscriptural doctrine of the Trinity," but rather in the Unity of God, and he honored Christ as a great teacher rather than as a divine being.

The American Unitarian Association had been founded in 1825 as a small publishing house for sermons, not as a denominational leadership group. Unitarian church leaders and congregants were men of affairs, well connected and well educated—the prosperous and urbane Boston Brahmins. But Unitarians were religiously complacent—choosing not to proselytize or actively convert others, in contrast to the aggressively expansive Congregationalist evangelicals.

The "Unitarian Controversy" was at its height at the time of Channing's speech. Many Congregationalist parishes "went Unitarian," and other congregations split into separate Congregational and Unitarian churches. Nine of Boston's ten Congregational churches became Unitarian, as did churches in all but three of the largest towns within twenty-five miles of Boston, including many of the oldest and strongest churches. By 1835, there were one hundred twenty-five Unitarian churches, and four hundred Congregational churches in New England. Both the Congregationalists and the Unitarians were congregational in governance, so Congregationalists distanced themselves from Unitarians by identifying their churches as Trinitarian Congregationalist. The label held for a century, and in 1890, Boston had twenty-six Unitarian churches and thirty-six Trinitarian Congregationalist churches.

Although the record is scanty, Boston's Society for Propagation of the Gospel would have been caught up in the conflict. More than two thirds of the society's Select Committee members before 1800 were clergy (and an even higher proportion thereafter), with half from Boston. While most represented churches that became Unitarian, some were notable Congregationalists whose churches remained in the Congregational fold. Conservative leader Jedidiah Morse was society secretary for the ten years from 1800 to 1810, a time when two famous early Unitarians—Channing and Ware—became members. The society initiated an annual public "discourse" in 1803, presented by a society clergyman until discontinued in 1835. Following the lead of a similar Massachusetts charitable group, conservatives and liberals originally delivered the society's annual address in alternate years; liberals, however, later dominated.

Ralph Waldo Emerson influenced Unitarian thought away from Christianity's past, its reliance on miracles, and its theology of the innate depravity of man. In his 1838 Divinity School Address, Emerson said that man is born "to the good, to the perfect," and God reveals religious truths directly to seekers. Soon after, Theodore Parker preached that the truth of Christianity does not rely on the infallibility of the Bible or the personal authority of Christ. A Christian, said Parker, is "he that is loving God and man and living in accordance with that love." Parker inflamed Unitarian leadership and launched a generation of controversy: Conservatives within Unitarian churches insisted on the authority of Christ, while Parker and the radicals held to the principle of free inquiry. The controversy brought denominational growth to a standstill.

In the meantime, in the increasingly humanitarian climate of New England, Congregationalism was moving toward emphasis on a loving, merciful God. Congregational churches grew, becoming less doctrinal, more active in social issues, and leaders in temperance, prison reform, and women's rights movements. As early as the 1840s, some Congregational churches split, with antislavery groups forming separate churches, and Congregationalists were a powerful voice for abolitionism in the years before the Civil War.

Unitarians tempered their internal dissent over time and became socially active, particularly as opponents of slavery. The growth of Unitarianism resumed after the Civil War, and through the latter years of the nineteenth century, Unitarianism became a national denomination. Unitarians still needed to tread lightly—at the time of the founding of the Unitarian church in Ithaca, New York, in 1865, "the trend in religious thought . . . made it necessary that the liberal movement proceed with as little shock as possible to the orthodox community."

By Thomas Elliott's time, the denomination was stronger and growing in influence, and summer meetings had become an important part of Unitarian strength at the turn of the century. Summer camp meetings and summer camps were a nineteenth century Protestant tradition. Historic summer camps like Chautauqua in New York state and Ocean Grove in New Jersey are still religious centers. Today many denominations support summer tent camps and more permanent facilities or hold summer retreats at public sites in rural settings.

Early Years
of the Summer Conferences

Thomas Elliott cast a wide net to recruit Unitarians, Congregationalists, and others for the 1897 meeting at Star Island. He reached beyond his own North Middlesex Conference of Unitarian Churches to other church conferences in New England to form the nondenominational Isles of Shoals Summer Meetings Association—almost immediately known as the Unitarian Summer Meetings Association. An advertisement for the first meeting gave "directions for those desiring to attend." Today's conferees who drive many miles to Portsmouth and crowd into the parking lot at the dock can be envious of Elliott's arrangements: "Check baggage through to Isles of Shoals, N.H. Go to Portsmouth, N.H., by the Eastern Division of the Boston & Maine, there take steamer 'Viking,' three or four minutes' walk from station."

Abby Jocquith was one of "Thomas Elliott's 600" (the number is variously given as 500 and 600) at that first conference, and she described the program at length in her local newspaper. Appropriately, the first morning's session spoke to Unitarian Vision and Inspiration, and the next morning a Congregationalist leader's topic was Consideration of Our Common Congregational Heritage and Sympathies. Other sessions presaged Star Island's future separate conference weeks—The Women's Alliance Work and Aims, The Sunday School and Its Interests, and a Young People's service.

A Celia Thaxter memorial service on Appledore Island during that first conference implicitly linked the intellectual tradition of Celia's parlor with future conferences at the Shoals. Many years later, Rutledge wrote with some hyperbole on the same theme: "From 1850 to 1900, literary and artistic celebrities had come . . . [to Appledore] whose climate and cultural atmosphere were conducive to creative work. Now with the advent of the Summer Meetings Association, people of the same high rank came . . . and Star Island developed into a cultural center of an even higher order."

The chapel's original wooden tower had blown down in 1892, and Oscar Laighton designed and built the stone tower that we see today. But, the Reverend Louis Cornish wrote, the first conferees found the chapel "in dilapidation." In Rutledge's description, "The interior had fallen into ruinous decay. The wooden steps at the north entrance and the wooden floor had rotted until it was hardly safe to enter . . . Plaster on the walls was dingy and broken. The opening which had been a door at the west end was left ragged and unplastered."

The 1923 publication of the Congregational Summer Meetings Association, *Brief History of the Isles of Shoals*, suggested that because the chapel had been built with funds raised by the Boston society, and the society had "come into the management of the Unitarians," the Star Island meeting house appropriately passed along to the use of the Unitarian conferences." However, Oscar Laighton seemed to have assumed that the town of Gosport's deed of the island's common lands to John Poor included the meetinghouse, and through the Laightons' purchase of the Oceanic Hotel, they also became owners the chapel. Oscar Laighton wrote, "They [the Unitarians] were so much interested in the old stone church that, with the consent of my brother's wife [Julia Laighton], I gave it to them." In actuality, Oscar Laighton leased the meetinghouse to the Summer Meetings Association with the stipulation that the tenants restore and maintain the building—an agreement that reflected early Unitarian conferees enthusiasm for a place of worship and the canniness of Oscar Laighton's business sense.

By the second conference, fundraising, led by Cornish, was underway for chapel restoration, and twelve hundred dollars was raised and the chapel "somewhat strengthened and improved." A brick floor was laid, the walls plastered, and window frames and roof repaired. Frederick T. McGill wrote in *Something Like a Star*, "William Roger Greeley, a young architecture student at one of the early conferences, stepped into the abandoned Gosport Meetinghouse" to determine what needed to be done to make it usable. "In a pile of rubble Roger found a wooden bracket with three branching arms that obviously fitted a spot on the wall, and he realized it was a hook for hanging lanterns. From this clue to the lighting arrangement sprang our traditional candlelight processions up and down the hill."

Services were held in the chapel starting in 1901, and the chapel became central to summer conferences. A large pulpit Bible was given to the Summer Meetings Association, still in the Vaughn Cottage collections. An organ replaced the chapel's earlier melodeon; the melodeon was placed in the Pink Parlor of the Oceanic Hotel and later moved to the hotel's Writing Room. The 1907 brochure for the Oceanic Hotel showed a photograph of the chapel with this caption: "Regular Sunday Services will be held in this ancient church during the season."

By 1903, the candlelight service was in print as *The Order of Evening Worship*, and the Isles of Shoals Association published *The Isles of Shoals*

Hymn Book and Candle Light Service in 1908. Some early conferees purchased copies, and occasionally a copy with an owner's bookplate is offered for sale on the Internet. The format of *The Isles of Shoals Hymn Book* differs from that of modern hymnbooks; the notes for four-part harmony were printed in musical staff form at the top of the page and two or three multi-verse hymns that could be used with the music were printed below. The introduction to the 1908 *Hymn Book and Candle Light Service* explained, "Hymns that breathe the spirit of the outdoor world, the tranquility of the season's withdrawal from the fret and custom of the busy world to be near to Nature's heart have been especially sought out."

The scripted candlelight service was an anomaly for Unitarian inheritors of the Puritans' repudiation of Prayer Book–based Anglicanism. While a modern Protestant service often has a short responsive reading, the candlelight service was, in its entirety, a responsive reading. Its text was loosely drawn from biblical sources, particularly Psalms and the Old Testament books of the prophets, and, like Unitarian hymns of the time, spoke to the glory of God, the goodness of men, and love and service to others. The candlelight service liturgy is no longer used, but the formal candlelight service was an evening tradition at Star Island's Unitarian conferences for at least a half-century. Frederick McGill, a Shoaler since the 1920s, wrote warmly of those services: "Instead of voicing their own thoughts in original creations of poetry or prose, the leaders in those earlier times refrained from uttering anything personal; they preferred to let the goodness, beauty, and truth of the liturgy speak for them."

For ten years, from 1897 to 1907, the Unitarian Summer Meeting Association held a one-week conference at the Shoals. The Unitarian Summer Meeting Association added a second week in 1908 for the Isles of Shoals Sunday School Institute. The Congregational Summer Conference Association was formed in 1914, and Congregationalists also held a one-week conference.

The Oceanic Hotel continued to be open to the public, and a 1902 advertisement in the *Portsmouth Daily Chronicle* directed at day-trippers announced "Regular Dinners in the Main Dining Room, $1.25, and First Rate Fish dinners at $.75 in the West Dining Room." The 1907 Oceanic Hotel brochure notes "steam heat and public and private bathrooms, and describes "the spacious ballroom, fitted with stage curtains and scenery . . . There are also a new cement tennis court and fine croquet grounds near the hotel." The large dining room was added soon after; a 1911 postcard features a view of the Oceanic dining room with chairs that are still in use nearly a century later.

Purchase of Star Island and the Oceanic Hotel

The Shoals hotels had been in their twilight years for some time, unable to compete with newer hotels, or with mainland hotels better serving "the changing tastes of pleasure seekers." The nearby Wentworth by the Sea offered riding stables, tennis, golf, and a saltwater lake "warmer than the frigid Atlantic." Cedric and Oscar Laighton continued trying to sell land on Appledore for cottages, but there was no longer interest in having a summer home there. Before Cedric Laighton's death, the brothers had mortgaged their Appledore land and hotel, and the bank foreclosed in 1900.

Smuttynose, Malaga and Duck Islands found a buyer in 1907. That year the bank called "the mortgage deed given by Oscar Laighton and Julia Laighton to the Piscataqua Savings Bank [on] Star Island, the hotel Oceanic and other buildings thereupon and all the personal property on the island used in conjunction with the hotel." The property was offered at public auction, and purchased by the bank for twenty-six hundred dollars. Oscar Laighton wrote, "The Appledore Hotel was being run by a syndicate at ever increasing loss. I was out of the business entirely . . . When my brother died I had thirty thousand dollars in my own right and a good brick house in Portsmouth; but in my effort to keep the interest on our indebtedness to the bank paid up, my fortune melted away and the fine house in town had to be sold."

The Appledore House burned to the ground in the fall of 1914, and Oscar Laighton spent his later years taking paying excursion parties around the islands in his motorboat, aptly named *Twilight*. Late in 1915, the bank tried to sell the Oceanic Hotel and Star Island. There were two interested parties—the Isles of Shoals Summer Meetings Association and a proprietor of roadhouses. Fearing that Star Island would become "a disorderly resort," Lewis Parkhurst, a Unitarian and Star Island conferee, stepped forward with a cash down payment. The Isles of Shoals Summer Meetings Association (Unitarian) and Congregational Summer Meetings Association had no state authorization to hold property, and so formed The Star Island Corporation as a holding company to own and operate Star Island. The corporation raised money to repay Parkhurst, complete the purchase, and make improvements to the deteriorating facilities.

Up to 1870, the Gosport villagers owned their homes and land, but John Poore bought their properties to assemble the land for his Oceanic Hotel, and, as noted, at the same time, the town of Gosport deeded its common land to Poor. Thus, the Laighton brothers' 1876 purchase of the Oceanic Hotel included all of Star Island, except for the land and houses of two villagers, which eventually came into Laighton hands. Bank foreclosures on the Laightons' notes had brought it into possession of the island, and as a result of the bank's sale, in 1916 the Star Island Corporation owned both the Oceanic Hotel and Star Island.

A bank still held Appledore Island, except for small parcels in private hands, and in 1922, James Donovan bought the bank's Appledore holdings. Donovan sold a few acres on Appledore Island to the Star Island Corporation in 1924, and the rest of his land to the corporation in 1929. Today, the Star Island Corporation owns Star Island and virtually all of Appledore Island except for a few private cottages. The State of New Hampshire owns White and Seavey Islands, Smuttynose and Malaga Islands are privately owned with public access under the control of the National Wildlife Service, Cedar and Lunging Islands are privately owned and not open to the public, and Duck Island is a nature preserve.

OCEANIC HOTEL

Summer Conferences of the 1920s and '30s

The Star Island Corporation dedicated the island in 1916 "to the glory of God and the well-being of Man; to the brotherhood of all earnest souls; to the untrammeled study and utterance of the truth; to the promotion of pure religion." The Star Island Religious and Educational Conference Center was formed in the spirit of Thomas Elliott's plan "to worship God here in the midst of His sea, to take counsel together of the deep things that abide, and to share the friendship and the hope of a common faith."

Four weeks of summer conferences were held at the Shoals during 1916, the Oceanic Hotel's first summer under Star Island Corporation management. The Isles of Shoals were closed to visitors during World War I, with conferences held on the mainland, but in 1919 conferees came again to Star Island. We have a detailed picture of the Unitarian summer conferences during the 1920s and '30s through Jessie E. Donahue's reporting in the *Boston Evening Transcript*, although she did not similarly write about the Congregational conference. Donahue had been involved in marshaling funds for the purchase of Star Island, and she was an active participant in summer conferences rather than a disinterested reporter.

The *Evening Transcript* was a major Boston newspaper from well before the Civil War until its demise on the eve of World War II. In its later years, the *Transcript* was an evening paper of soft news, particularly known for its weekly genealogical column and read by Old Boston. T. S. Eliot's short poem titled "The Boston Evening Transcript," characterized the newspaper's readership in a few lines:

> *. . . evening quickens faintly in the street,*
> *Wakening the appetites of life in some*
> *And to others bringing the* Boston Evening Transcript *. . .*

In an age when metropolitan daily newspapers seldom print denominational news, it comes as a surprise to see the extent of Donahue's coverage of the Unitarian summer conferences in the *Boston Evening Transcript*. This was a period when attendees often stayed for a number of weeks. The Shoaler

84

recording the chapel bell failure in 1924 was on Star Island for a month, attending Institute for Religious Education, Alliance Week, and the General Conference. In the early years, the Shoals General Conference was considered the serious conference, and brought nationally prominent Unitarian ministers as speakers, each for a single address to the group as a whole. Donahue reported their sermons at length, mostly on theological issues specific to Unitarianism.

By 1929, the schedule of summer conferences had evolved to nine weeks, with two weeks apiece for Young People's Religious Union, Shoals General Conference, and the Congregational Conference, and one week for the Religious Education Institute, Women's Alliance, and a "No Program Week." The evolution of the Star Island conferences is comprehensively described in the section "100 Years of Religious Conferences on Star Island" in the seventh edition of Rutledge's *Ten Miles Out*, published in 1997.

The Sunday School Institute was a professional development program for teachers in the church school, as the Religious Education Conference continues to be today. Early programs were under the auspices of the Unitarian Sunday School Society, and "teachers and Sunday School workers were sent to the Institute at the expense of their church, the Alliance, or Sunday School." The Sunday School Institutes introduced new curricula, with an emphasis on crafts and, for a time, pageants and, in 1928, a Model Church School Class for children of conferees.

Speakers at the Sunday School Institute (later the Religious Education Institute) brought changing views on psychology and reflected an evolving philosophy of childhood education. An article describing the first Sunday School Institute in 1908 was headlined "Many Very Radical Changes Needed. The Old Testament Use in the Education of the Child—A Call for Less of It and a Different Manner of Presentation—Too Much 'Monster' God and Too Little Moral Spirit."

The Women's Alliance was the largest of the 1920s conferences. Pageants were popular, and a series of annual pageants featured Old Testament prophets, including Hosea, Ezekiel, and Amos. The Amos pageant of 1929 was held out on the rocks at sunrise; a photograph shows Amos dressed in robes and carrying a shepherd's staff. A 1934 pageant, "Ninety-five Years at the Shoals," honored Oscar Laighton. The one hundredth anniversary of Celia Thaxter's birth was celebrated in 1935 by reproducing her Appledore Island flower garden on Star Island (where it did not flourish) and with a pageant, with, as Donahue described her, "Mrs. Thaxter picking flowers and strolling among her flower beds gowned in a white costume." One morning, reported Donahue, Alliance women went "deep sea fishing for cod and pollock at 5:30 a.m." Musicale participants were listed, one year playing "compositions by Tchaikovsky, Bizet, Sibelius, and Beethoven," and the person reading the evening's "traditional candlelight service in the meeting-house" always named.

The two-week Young People's Religious Union conference drew an increasingly large and enthusiastic group of twenty-to-thirty-year-olds. Donahue regularly reported YPRU sports activities, and, once, a sunrise swim with young people "cavorting in 53 degree water." There was an annual stunt night with "clever and original stunts," and YPRUers made much sport of the bell that clanged flat after its 1924 repair, replicating the sound of the bell by clanging pot lids. Each year Donahue told readers about the YPRU "best song contest," with new Shoals-related lyrics written for well-known tunes of the day—often won by Frederick McGill. These are the songs in the *Star Island Song Book*, still used for Banquet Night at many conferences, although today few conferees know the tunes.

Frederick McGill first attended the YPRU conference in 1922, its second year, and Virginia Frederick who would later marry him, came for the first time a year later. In the couple's book, *Something Like a Star: A Rather Personal View of the Star Island Conference Center*, McGill reflected on his many years of YPRU conferences: "Those of us who attended the youth weeks for ten or more seasons just had to pick up gleanings of theology and ethics that would give deeper meaning to later experiences in literature and life. We also found—if we had not already discovered it—that ministers were people, and that many of them could be hilariously funny."

Thomas Elliott had envisioned that the Isles of Shoals Summer Meetings Association would bring together Unitarian clergy and laymen, in part to strengthen the growing Unitarian church. "Star Island Chronicles," a newsletter of the 1916 Unitarian conferences, listed the two hundred fifty individuals in attendance that year, and quite a few were *Reverend and Mrs. __*. McGill's words lend credence to the effectiveness of this practice.

Donahue's articles chronicled island improvements during her twenty years of reporting. In 1920, "ministers, laymen, and laywomen" put a "fresh coat of white paint on the chapel woodwork, including the bell tower," the chapel bell was replaced in 1931, and in 1935 the Women's Alliance reconditioned the chapel organ. The wood parsonage had burned in 1905, and in 1927, Reverend Lyman V. Rutledge led a group of "Ministers of our

Fellowship" in funding and building a stone parsonage, Star Island's only new building until after World War II. Rutledge noted that the islanders had always called the home of their minister a "parsonage," while *manse* was a term used elsewhere in New England. In the same vein, another minister of this era deplored the increasing references to Star Island's "chapel," saying that it should be called *meetinghouse* instead.

Later Conferences

During World War II, there was no public access to the Isles of Shoals, and Unitarian conferences were held for four summers at a New Hampshire lake. Conferences returned to Star Island in 1946. After World War II, the Star Island facilities were in poor condition having had virtually no maintenance during the Depression and because of their vacancy during the war. A major campaign financed necessary kitchen and power-generation infrastructure, and, as conferences began to schedule more concurrent activities, provided for group meeting places in addition to the Oceanic Hotel's Elliott and Lawrance Halls.

At the time that the stone Tucke Parsonage was built, the Increased Accommodations at Star Island Committee anticipated building any new structures of stone and the eventual replacement of all wooden buildings. William Roger Greeley, the architect for many of the buildings, drew up a plan for the Stone Village, and the first postwar buildings were of stone. Asa Merrick Parker Memorial Hall was built in 1948; funded by Congregational Shoalers, it housed a meeting room. The Newton Centre Unitarian Church funded Star Island's Newton Centre Parish House; built in 1950, it had two meeting rooms. The 1960 Vaughn Memorial Building included the Charles F. Vaughn Reading Room and the Celia Thaxter Room, a small museum. Marshman, with a public meeting room, was built in 1998—the only new stone building in nearly forty years. A longtime Shoaler from Life On A Star conferences donated the funds for the building as a memorial to Barbara Marshman, a Unitarian Universalist religious educator who was a Religious Education conferee.

As conference sizes grew and more guest and program rooms were needed, it became impractical to continue building in stone, necessitating less expensive construction of wood. Sprague and Founders cottages were built in 1953, and YPRU and Baker cottages in 1955, with Sprague, YPRU, and Baker linked to the Oceanic Hotel by an extension of its veranda. A barn was converted in 1965 for use with children's groups as the Kiddie Barn, and the old icehouse became the Art Barn in 1970. The Dement Infirmary was built in 1967, and the Douglas H. Brookfield Youth Center and Lyman V. Rutledge Marine Science Laboratory constructed in 1971. Louise's Barn, a facility for groups of younger children completed in 2003, was named after a Shoaler who was a marine biologist on the founding faculty of the Shoals Marine Lab and a long-time Religious Education conferee.

Family conferences had been inaugurated in 1940 with the All Star

Conference, designed for YPRU alumni and billed as a conference for Unitarians twenty-five to fifty years of age, with "arrangements for children." During World War II, this conference was not one of those held on the mainland, so the next All Star Conference took place in 1946. The All Star Conference flourished, and an All Star II conference was added in 1957. A third family conference, Life On A Star (LOAS), began in 1963, with LOAS II added the next year. Congregational conferences became family conferences as well. "The family weeks," McGill wrote, "continue to bring two very special bonuses to the Island; assurance of financial stability by reason of capacity attendance at every Conference, and loyalty and devotion from the children who will grow to love the Island and their Island friends, and so will keep the Star connection all their lives."

The Religious Education Conference (RE) continues to this day in its original mission of strengthening the church school program of mainland churches. Thomas Elliott's original Summer Meeting became the Shoals General Conference in 1924. The program became more secular and increasingly focused on world affairs, and in 1948 was renamed the World Order Conference, becoming the International Affairs Conference ten years later. The Institute on Religion in an Age of Science (IRAS) was founded in 1954 as a Star Island conference for religious people and scientists to find common ground. In addition to the summer conference, IRAS is a year-round organization of scholars, and publishes a quarterly journal, *Zygon*. McGill called the two weeks of IRAS and International Affairs conferences "the most intellectually stimulating fortnight of the season."

Through the years, a number of smaller special interest conferences have been added, and now share weeks or parts of weeks in the early and later portions of summer. In June 2004, the Arts Conference shared part of its week with the Young Adults Conference and the rest with the Isles of Shoals Historical and Research Association (ISHRA) Conference. The Natural History Conference and the Young Religious Unitarian Universalists shared the next week. During two weeks in August, each of the United Church of Christ Family Conferences shared a week with a UCC Youth Conference. Near the end of the summer, there were two weekend conferences, the UCC Weekend Conference of the Laity and Labor Day weekend's Pelican Reunion. The end-of-season staff provided limited service to small September conference groups—Midweek Retreats, weekend Star Island Women's groups, a writing group and a photography group, a second ISHRA conference, and two Elderhostels.

The University of New Hampshire (UNH) from 1928 through 1940 ran the Appledore School of Marine Zoology in Appledore Island cottages that survived the 1914 fire, offering undergraduate and graduate summer courses under the direction of Professor C. F. Jackson. Marine science education returned to the Shoals when Dr. John Kingsbury, of Cornell University, was invited to Star Island as speaker for the 1964 LOAS conference. The next summer, a biologist was added to the Star Island staff, and Lawrance Hall in the Oceanic Hotel was converted into a marine laboratory with saltwater trays and large tanks in preparation for an academic program utilizing the rich marine life of Shoals waters.

Kingsbury worked with Cornell and UNH to offer a four-week Field Marine Science college course, with two weeks in the Lawrance Hall laboratory at Star Island and two weeks in a UNH facility. In 1971, the program moved to Star Island's new Rutledge Marine Science Laboratory. Under Kingsbury's leadership, a marine field research station was built at Appledore Island on land leased by Cornell from the Star Island Corporation. In 1973, Cornell and UNH opened the Shoals Marine Laboratory, offering a full summer of programming for college students as well as for teachers and the public. Star Island's Rutledge Marine Laboratory continues to be staffed by a biologist, and there conference children are introduced to the wonders of ocean life.

Major mid-century denominational changes affected both Congregationalists and Unitarians. In 1957, the Congregational Christian Church and the Evangelical and Reformed Church—groups with origins dating to early Reformed churches in Europe—merged as the United Church of Christ, "a community of faith that seeks to respond to the Gospel of Jesus Christ in word and deed," and today is in the forefront of social-justice issues. Earlier mergers had brought together the Congregational Church and Christian Churches. Similarly, the Reformed Churches in the United States earlier joined with the Evangelical Synod of North America, a denomination growing out of the 1817 union of Lutheran and Reformed churches in Germany.

The Unitarians and Universalists merged in 1961, becoming the Unitarian Universalist Association. The Unitarian heritage of the UUs traces its origins to sixteenth and seventeenth century Unitarian congregations in Transylvania and Poland, eighteenth century English Unitarians, and American Unitarianism's origin in New England Congregationalism. Universalism predated Unitarianism by a few years as a denomination separate from Congregationalism. Universalism was a rural counterpart to urban Unitarianism, and, similarly, a liberal response to the evangelistic conservatism of the Second Great Awakening. Universalists rejected the concept of God's condemnation of humans to eternal damnation, believing instead that all people will be saved. In the nineteenth century, Universalists were greater in number than Unitarians, but at the time of the merger, Unitarians were the larger group.

The Star Island Corporation's strategic plan "Reaffirms the centrality of the Unitarian Universalist Association and the United Church of Christ spiritual traditions." The Star Island Corporation, a nonprofit membership organization drawn from all the conferences, elects a governing board and, like the original board of 1916, board members proportionally represent Unitarian Universalist and United Church of Christ conferences. The Unitarian Summer Meetings Association continues today as the Isles of Shoals Association, Unitarian Universalist, Inc. (ISAUU), "dedicated to promoting the spirit and traditions of religious and education programs at the Isles of Shoals." The Congregational Summer Meetings Association is now the Star Island United Church of Christ (SIUCC). The ISAUU and SIUUC presidents sit *ex officio* on the Star Island Corporation board, as they have since its incorporation in 1916.

The ISAUU recently initiated a Clergy Grants program, funding room-and-board expenses for UU ministers and their families who have not yet attended a Star Island conference. The Association sees the Clergy Grants program as a direct outgrowth of Thomas Elliott's original vision for the conferences, and the practice continues the ecumenical spirit that pervaded all his early organizational work. The ISUAA also gives an amount representing 10 percent of the total clergy grants to support the SIUCC Scholarship Fund.

The ISAUU undertook an extensive renovation of the chapel 1977. The chapel was "stripped to the bones," and its walls replastered and re-white-washed. The tower foundation was strengthened, and the woodwork, window trim, and pews painted with a modern formulation of the original milk paint made by mixing brick dust with cow's milk and lacquer. The Star Island Corporation, ISAUU, and SIUCC worked together on another renovation in 2005. Outside contractors extensively repaired the bell tower and reroofed the chapel, and volunteers repaired and repainted interior walls and the brick red woodwork, window shutters, and pews.

Star Island Today

It is a point of pride to Shoalers that the Oceanic Hotel looks the same to conferees docking at the Star Island pier today as it did more than a century ago to Thomas Elliott's friends arriving for the first Summer Meeting. In addition to the old hotel, four handsome and well-proportioned white clapboard houses—those "white and square" buildings of Celia Thaxter's writings—lend historical authenticity to island atmosphere. Two smaller houses are believed to be the oldest houses still standing on the island. The Star Island Corporation's Strategic Plan notes, "Star Island preserves its nineteenth century appearance, charm and simplicity."

The hotel's guest rooms seem unchanged—there are shared bathrooms on each floor, bedroom lighting is a single bulb hanging from the ceiling, a pitcher of hot water is delivered to the door each morning, and conferees can shower twice a week in the Oceanic's lower-level shower room. In the words of the Conference Brochure, "Life is comfortable, but not modern." Thus, attendees are those who value the intellectual, religious, and spiritual aspects of Star Island conferences over first-class hotel accommodations. Food is excellent, but Shoalers particularly enjoy the variety and congeniality of tablemates for family-style meals at tables for ten in the Oceanic dining room. The Oceanic Hotel does not sell or serve alcoholic beverages, but there is a conference-sponsored predinner social hour most weeks.

As the Conference Brochure puts it, "Shoalers old and new come to Star Island to enjoy and be inspired by its windswept cliffs, wildflower-laden paths, historic buildings and cemeteries, and ever-changing ocean views." Similarly, 130 years earlier, Jenness wrote that people "come yearly . . . to refresh their jaded spirits in the cool solitude, the healing silence, of these barren rocks." Many conference activities focus on the island environment, and attendees are out-of-doors much of the time. Geology, low-tide, and bird walks are scheduled for many conferences, the large front lawn invites people of all ages to play, and conferees chat or read on the porch in Star Island's signature rocking chairs. Many find spirituality in closeness to island sunshine, winds, storms, and the ever-changing ocean.

The Star Island Corporation runs the island's facilities, and board and corporation members are volunteers. The board hires an executive director along with a small year-round staff. The board and its committees work with the executive director and staff to run the hotel and manage the facilities. The Star Island Corporation has an office in Portsmouth; only an island caretaker is at the Shoals during the winter.

While much is constant in the island's appearance and in the conferee experience, recently there have been major infrastructure improvements. Environmental regulations necessitated installation of a waste-water treatment plant, with its challenges of bacterial decomposition in seawater. Reverse osmosis water-making technology has been installed so the hotel is no longer dependent on water from the mainland. Ramps have made a number of buildings accessible to those with curtailed mobility. Upgraded kitchen, dishwashing, and laundry equipment and space have increased food preparation and housekeeping efficiency, and ever-improving generator capacity provides electricity. The pier has been extensively rebuilt after major hurricane damage.

Safety infrastructure and enforcement receive particular attention. A sprinkler system in the old wooden buildings, smoke alarms throughout, a second fireproof internal stairway for the Oceanic Hotel, and two fireproof stairway towers in the Gosport section of the Oceanic have been significant investments. Employees are specially trained in fire and rescue techniques, and a fire drill is held during every conference. The first day's mandatory "fire and water talk" is a longtime feature of each conference. Attendees chuckle as the island manager explains "three kinds of water"—seawater in the toilets, cistern water for showers, and drinking water. The island manager is emphatic that there must be no smoking in either guestrooms or public rooms, and no illegal drug use at all; the penalty is immediate expulsion from the island.

The island's capacity is 250 to 265 conferees, depending on the number of small children in their parents' room and the need for single-occupancy rooms. Star Island also houses one hundred staff members. Most are college-age Pelicans, a name dating from the 1930s. Many Pelicans have been coming to Star Island conferences since childhood. The island manager works closely with the Pels to ensure that their experience is worthwhile, conference speakers often meet with the young people, and Pelicans have their own chapel services.

The traditional Pelican job titles are colorful: Pels are waitrae and chamber (formerly waitress and chambermaid), cook, baker, butter cutter, kitchie, dishie (dishwasher), laundry (laundry worker), snackie (snack bar assistant), painter, carp (carpenter), truckie (truck crew), dockie (waterfront staff), engineer, deskie (hotel front desk worker), night crew, and rounder (a substitute who fills in as needed). Pelican traditions include a weekly Pelican-Conferee softball game and on Lobster Night, the waitrae walk arm-in-arm across the lawn and, still clothed, into the water. Pelicans present a Pel Show at each conference, with songs, original skits, and the Pel Chorus and its rousing "Star Island Is Our Spirit's Home."

Each conference is an autonomous and self-perpetuating entity, and registration is through that conference's registrar. First-time conferees (called New Shoalers) are welcomed, and Old Shoalers honored—many attendees have been coming to Star Island for more than fifty years, often returning each year to the same conference. Memorably, Pels greet arriving conferees at the dock, chanting, "You did come back." After a conference, Pels see off departing conferees with, "You will come back," and as the boat pulls away from the dock, Shoalers on board respond, "We will come back."

Conferences combine a religious or spiritual focus with an educational one, and each conference has its own climate, culture, and traditions. The topic of the week may be literary, scientific, sociological, or a national or international issue, and there are often suggested readings. Conference leaders establish the conference topic of the week, secure a speaker, and ask other conferees to take on many of the conference responsibilities. Almost everyone has a participatory role, large or small, and many have an opportunity to share their talents, interests, and expertise.

The Children's Program is central to family conferences. Children join others their age each morning and afternoon as Nestlings, Starlings, Puffins, Terns, Gulls, Junior Teens, or Senior Teens. They are introduced to the Shoals marine environment, Star Island's geology and birdlife, and the lore and legends of the Shoals. The Art Barn is a favorite, and conferee musicians share music with young people. There is a daily Children's Chapel, and each group is part of Children's Stunt Night and at some conferences, Senior Teens present the Thursday-evening chapel service. Parents and children spend time together and with other families, and value family "quality time" at Star Island.

Religion is integral to the conference experience. There is no denominational requirement for participants, but most are active in mainland congregations and come to Star Island with an expectation of being part of a weeklong religious community. Each conference chooses its own minister of the week who leads some of the chapel services and offers pastoral care to attendees and staff, and the Star Island Corporation provides a scholarship for each conference minister of the week and his or her partner. Conferees honor Star Island's religious traditions, its climate of retreat, and the chapel as a sacred space. The chapel is always open, and the evening chapel service brings closure to each day.

The Star Island evening chapel service is unique. Conferees, already quiet and contemplative, gather in darkness on the long porch of the Oceanic Hotel overlooking Gosport Harbor. The chapel bell starts ringing and a line of Shoalers moves toward the end of the porch, where every other person picks up a lighted lantern, its candle protected from the wind by a glass chimney. By lantern light and sometimes moonlight, Shoalers walk in silence up the path to the two-century-old stone chapel and enter to the music of the small old organ. Shoalers hang lanterns on the three-pronged wall brackets and a soft glow suffuses the chapel. A conferee or minister leads a short chapel service—words of meditation, a message, perhaps with congregational participation, and a hymn accompanied by the old organ. As the service ends, Shoalers take their lanterns and walk down the path, still silent until returning lanterns to the porch.

Shoalers value the sacredness of the candlelight service, a part of Star Island summer conferences for more than a century. Memories linger of those who worshipped in the stone chapel for a century before that, of those worshipping in earlier wood meetinghouses on the same high point of Star Island, and of those worshipping in an even earlier brick meetinghouse at the Shoals. And the words of the Reverend Louis Cornish, who led one of the chapel's first candlelight services, still ring true: "In silence depart, the beauty of the night and the murmur of the sea sealing us with a sense of our unity of purpose and of God's peace."

CANDLELIGHT PROCESSION TO STAR ISLAND CHAPEL

Acknowledgments

It was the Reverend Lyman V. Rutledge's histories that sparked my interest in Shoals religion, particularly his list "Isles of Shoals Ministers, Missionaries, Teachers, and Agents, 1637–1871," with asterisks denoting those appointed by the Society for Propagating the Gospel Among Indians and Others in North America. The title of one of Rutledge's books, *The Isles of Shoals in Lore and Legend* (1965), suggests stories of pirates, ghosts, murders, and life at the islands' Victorian summer hotels, and all are in its pages, but Rutledge was at heart a historian, and *Lore and Legend* is more history than tall tales.

Rutledge was a thorough researcher, uncovering Shoals history from old documents and out-of-print histories, compiling a useful chronology, and providing extensive bibliographies so others could follow. Rutledge's trail led to *The Isles of Shoals: An Historical Sketch,* an 1873 book by John Scribner Jenness—in Rutledge's words, "the first authentic history of the Shoals." Later authors, including Rutledge, quoted at length Jenness's history of colonial and post-Revolutionary War periods. Indeed, much that has been written about the first two centuries at the Shoals was taken verbatim from the second edition (1875) of the Jenness book, in an era when there was no compunction about using the words of another as one's own without attribution. I, too, quote Jenness frequently; his phrases reflect the cadence and perspective of his time and seem right for the topic.

Jenness had access to the town records of Gosport, available on Star Island through much of the nineteenth century. The town records and part of the church records, by then at the New Hampshire Historical Society, were transcribed by Dr. Joseph W. Warren and published for a wider audience in the 1912, 1913, and 1914 volumes of the *New England Historical & Genealogical Register.* Through the kindness of Laurance Bussey of the Isles of Shoals Historical and Research Association (ISHRA), I was privileged to read his photocopy of the complete manuscript of the Gosport church records.

Three other authors were Shoals residents for nearly a lifetime, and their works supplement and extend the Jenness history through the period of the great summer hotels. Celia Laighton Thaxter's *Among the Isles of Shoals* (1873) has been the most widely read depiction of the Shoals and its people, and is particularly of value for her description of Gosport in its last days as a town. Oscar Laighton's *Ninety Years at the Isles of Shoals* (1930) spanned his time before, during, and after the Victorian summer resort era, including the building of the Oceanic Hotel, its acquisition by the Laightons, and Oscar Laighton's loss of his Shoals hotels to bankruptcy. Cedric Laighton's correspondence with his sister was edited and published by Frederick T. McGill as *Letters to Celia*. Cedric's letters written from 1860 through 1875 describe the Laightons' annual expansion of their hotel facilities and the John Poor purchase of Star Island. Celia Thaxter's granddaughter Rosamond Thaxter based her 1966 biography of Celia Thaxter, *Sandpiper*, on family records and memories.

Sources for the summer religious conference years include a second Rutledge book, *Ten Miles Out: Guide Book to the Isles of Shoals*, first published in 1949 and regularly updated, most recently (1997) with revisions and additions by his son Edward F. Rutledge, and now the most comprehensive summary of the evolution of Star Island Conferences. McGill and his wife, Virginia F. McGill, recalled their years as Star Island conferees and staff members in *Something Like a Star: A Rather Personal View of the Star Island Conference Center* (1989).

I was privileged to have access to documents from the files of the Vaughn Cottage Museum at Star Island. Sally Sapienza, the 2004 curator, jump-started my project by locating and photocopying the typed transcripts listed in the bibliography and sharing the Jessie E. Donahue *Boston Evening Transcript* articles. The 2005 curator, Melissa Saggerer, found additional materials for me, including early brochures of the Oceanic Hotel. Joy Thurlow Leclair, a Caswell descendant, provided information about the Caswell family and the Caswell family cemetery. I also used the many recent publications about the Isles of Shoals that are available at the Star Island Bookstore and in Portsmouth bookshops.

I visited the Portsmouth Athenaeum to read extant reports of the Newburyport Society for Promoting Religious Instruction at the Isles of Shoals. I found the 1914 and 1916 pamphlets, "Dedication of a Memorial to Reverend John Tucke" at the Portsmouth Public Library, and *The Tyng Family in America* at the Historical Society of Old Newbury in Newburyport, where Jay Williamson talked with me about early Newburyport and Marge Motes located references to Dudley A. Tyng's work at the Shoals in *The History of Newburyport*.

The Internet was not available to earlier researchers. The "Brief Account of the Boston Society for Propagating the Gospel Among the Indians and

Others in North America" (1798) was on the Internet, as were five of the society's reports of the 1840s. Internet sleuthing yielded additional information about the Reverends Richard Gibson, Joseph Hull, Josiah Moody, Samuel Belcher, John Tucke, Jedidiah Morse, Andrew Peabody, and George Beebe, and Dudley A. Tyng as well as the topics of the Anglicans, the Puritans, the Gorges and Mason charters, the fishery monopoly, Navigation Acts, Congregational Church, religious revivals in New England, the Unitarian Controversy, and the Star Island Corporation.

Bobby Williams, my son, graciously provided the illustrations that accompany the text as well as the cover photograph. Bobby was an integral part of the research for this project—he identified and helped obtain rare documents, including the 1875 Jenness book, a reprint of "The Autobiographical Memoranda of John Brock," and *The Churches of Rye, New Hampshire, 1725–1959* by John L. Parsons. Bobby drew on his deep knowledge of world history to provide valuable insight to important historical points, as did my brother, Donald Crane, a Maine historian and poet.

Irene Bush, president of the Star Island Corporation, offered suggestions on the "Star Island Today" section. Donna Titus, an artist, writer, island historian, and active ISHRA member, and Suzy Mansfield, Star Island chapel historian and an officer of the Isles of Shoals Association, Unitarian Universalist, Inc., reviewed the manuscript for historical accuracy, and Suzy Mansfield told me the story of the YRPU chapel bell skits. Reverend Charles Close, a United Church of Christ minister serving the Wilbraham United Church, Massachusetts and frequent Star Island minister of the week, and Reverend Roger Fritz, minister of Cedar Lane Unitarian Universalist Church, in Bethesda, Maryland, critiqued early versions of the denominational history sections. Long-time Shoaler Lynn Stewart Shaffer carefully edited the manuscript, and Doris Troy was its conscientious copyeditor. I am grateful for the interest and helpful assistance from all these people.

I am appreciative of the Reverend Bradford Greeley, a retired Unitarian Universalist minister now in Portsmouth and vice president of the Isles of Shoals Corporation, for his foreword, affirming anew the importance of religion to Shoalers through the centuries. Lastly, I honor my husband, Peter Williams, who in 1975 convinced me that a Star Island conference would be a fine family experience. We brought Jane, Gilbert, Katherine, Annie, Louise, and later Bobby to the island, and we have ever since been Shoalers. Thirty years later, Peter encouraged my efforts to present an important aspect of Shoals history to the Shoals community.

Bibliography

Books and Articles

Bardwell, John D. *The Isles of Shoals: A Visual History.* Portsmouth, N.H.: Peter E. Randall Publisher, 1989.

Bigelow, E. Victor. *Brief History of the Isles of Shoals.* Congregational Summer Meetings Association, 1923.

Bremer, Francis J. *The Puritan Experiment: New England Society from Bradford to Edwards.* St. Martin's Press, 1976; Hanover, N.H.: University Press of New England, 1995.

Brother Anthony of Padua, F.M.S. *The Tyng Family in America.* Poughkeepsie, N.Y.: Marist Press, 1956.

"Church Membership, Marriages, and Baptisms on the Isles of Shoals in the Eighteenth Century" (transcribed by Joseph W. Warren) in *New England Historical & Genealogical Register*, 141–155, 209–225, 294–306. Vol. 66 (1912).

"Congregational Churches and Ministers in Rockingham County" in *New England Historical & Genealogical Register*, 256–258. Vol. 1 (1847).

Cooke, George Willis. *Unitarianism in America.* Boston: American Unitarian Association, 1902.

Currier, John J. *The History of Newburyport, Massachusetts, 1764–1905.* Vol. 1, 1906, vol. 2, 1909; facsimile edition, 1977.

Downs, John W. *Sprays of Salt.* Privately published, 1944. Reissued as *Sprays of Salt: Reminiscences of a Native Shoaler.* Portsmouth, N.H.: Peter E. Randall Publisher, 1997.

Emmet, Alan. "On the Isles of Shoals: Celia Thaxter and Her Garden by the Sea" in *So Fine a Prospect: Historic New England Gardens,* 130–143. Hanover, N.H.: University Press of New England, 1996.

Gage, William Leonard. *The Isles of Shoals in Summer Time.* Hartford, Conn, 1875.

Hammond, Otis Grant, ed. "Dedication of a Memorial to Reverend John Tucke, 1702–1773." New Hampshire Historical Society, 1914 and 1916.

Jenness, John Scribner. *The Isles of Shoals: An Historical Sketch.* New York, 1873 and 1875.

Laighton, Oscar. *Ninety Years at the Isles of Shoals.* Reprint of the Beacon Press 1930 edition, Boston: The Star Island Corporation, 1971.

Lawrence, Robert F. *New Hampshire Churches: Comprising Histories of Congregational and Presbyterian Churches in the State.* 1856.

MacCulloch, Diarmaid. *The Reformation.* New York: Penguin Books, 2003.

Mandel, Norma H. *Beyond the Garden Gate: The Life of Celia Laighton Thaxter*. Hanover, N.H.: University Press of New England, 2004.

Marlowe, George F. *Churches of Old New England: Their Architecture and Their Architects, Their Pastors and Their People*. New York: Macmillan Co., 1947.

Marsden, George M. *Jonathan Edwards: A Life*. New Haven, Conn.: Yale University Press, 2003.

Mather, Cotton. *Magnalia Christi Americana*. London, 1702. Reprinted by S. Andrus & Son, 1853.

McCusker, John J. and Russell R. Menard. *The Economy of British America, 1607–1789*. Chapel Hill: The University of North Carolina Press, 1991.

McGill, Frederick T. Jr. ed. *Letters to Celia*. Boston: The Star Island Corporation, 1972; reprinted, Portsmouth, N.H.: Peter E. Randall Publisher, 1996.

McGill, Frederick T. Jr. and Virginia F. McGill. *Something Like a Star: A Rather Personal View of the Star Island Conference Center*. Boston: The Star Island Corporation, 1989.

Parsons, Langdon Brown. *History of Rye, N.H.* First edition, 1905; reprinted, nd.

Penrose, Charles, Jr. "'They Live on a Rock in the Sea!' The Isles of Shoals in Colonial Times." Newcomen Society of North America, 1957.

Randall, Peter E. and Maryellen Burke. *Gosport Remembered: The Last Village at the Isle of Shoals*. Portsmouth, N.H.: Peter E. Randall Publisher, 1997.

Rapaport, Diane. "The Smuttynose Sailor Who Became a Judge" in *New England Ancestors*, 48–49. New England Historic Genealogical Society, Summer 2004.

Robinson, J. Dennis. *Wentworth by the Sea: The Life and Times of a Grand Hotel*. Portsmouth, N.H.: Peter E. Randall Publisher, 2004.

Rutledge, Lyman V. *Ten Miles Out: Guide Book to the Isles of Shoals, Portsmouth, New Hampshire*. First edition, Boston: The Star Island Corporation, 1949; seventh edition with revisions and additions by Edward F. Rutledge, Portsmouth, N.H.: Peter E. Randall Publisher, 1997.

Rutledge, Lyman V. *The Isles of Shoals in Lore and Legend*. Boston: The Star Island Corporation, 1971.

Shipton, Clifford K. "The Autobiographical Memoranda of John Brock, 1636–1659." Reprinted from *Proceedings of the American Antiquarian Society*, April 1943.

Stearns, Frank Preston. "Appledore and Its Visitors" in *Sketches from Concord and Appledore*, 223–252. New York: G. P. Putnam's Sons, 1895.

Titus, Donna Marion. *By This Wing: Letters by Celia Thaxter to Bradford Torrey about birds at the Isles of Shoals 1888 to 1894*. Manchester, N.H.: J. Palmer Publisher, nd.

Tregaris, Sharon, "On the Waterfront at the Shoals Marine Lab" in *Cornell Alumni News*, 54–58. 2005.

Thaxter, Celia. *Among the Isles of Shoals*. Facsimile reprint of 1873 edition, Wake-Brook House, Cape Cod, MA, nd.

Thaxter, Rosamond. *Sandpiper: The Life and Letters of Celia Thaxter*. First edition, 1963; fifth printing, Portsmouth, N.H.: Peter E. Randall Publisher, 1999.

"The Isles of Shoals" in *Harper's New Monthly Magazine*, 663–676. New York: Harper & Brothers, 1874.

"The Town Records of Gosport, N.H." (transcribed by Joseph W. Warren) in *New England Historical & Genealogical Register*, 56–63, 132–147, 231–248, 354–359 and 32–46, 127–142. Vol. 67 (1913); vol. 68 (1914).

University Art Galleries. *A Stern and Lovely Scene: A Visual History of the Isles of Shoals*. Durham, N.H.: University of New Hampshire, 1982.

Vallier, Jane E. *Poet on Demand: The Life, Letters, and Works of Celia Thaxter*. Camden, Maine: Down East Books, 1982;Portsmouth, N.H.: Peter E. Randall Publisher, 1994.

Weis, Frederick Lewis. *The Colonial Clergy and the Colonial Churches of New England*. Society of the Descendants of the Colonial Clergy, 1936; reprinted, Baltimore: The Genealogical Company, 1997.

Whittaker, Robert H. *Land of Lost Content: The Piscataqua River Basin and the Isles of Shoals. The People, Their Dreams, Their History*. Dover, N.H.: Alan Sutton Publishing Inc., 1993.

Williamson, William D. *The History of Maine from Its Discovery to Its Separation, 1602–1820*. Hallowell, Maine: 1832.

Wright, Conrad. *Three Prophets of Religious Liberalism: Channing, Emerson, Parker*. Boston: Beacon Press, 1961.

Documents at Vaughn Cottage at Star Island or the Portsmouth Anthenaeum

Alden, Rev. L. "Gosport." Typed manuscript of excerpt from Robert E. Lawrence. *New Hampshire Churches Comprising Histories of Congregational and Presbyterian Churches in the State*. 1856.

"Baptism of Shoals Children by Rev. Theophilus Cotton of Hampton Falls, N.H." Typed transcript of excerpt from "Records of Mr. Cotton" in the second volume of the *History of Hampton Falls, N.H.* nd.

Charlton, Edwin. "Church." Typed transcript of excerpt from *New Hampshire As It Is,* 1855.

Cornish, Louis C. 'The Story of the Isles of Shoals: An address delivered on Star Island, July 15, 1916, upon the occasion of the twentieth anniversary of the Unitarian Summer Meetings." Boston: Isles of Shoals Unitarian Summer Meetings Association, 1916; revised and enlarged, 1936.

Dana, Richard Henry Jr. "Vacation Ramble to Shoals." Typed manuscript of 1843 diary.

Donahue, Jessie E. *Boston Evening Transcript* articles about Star Island Unitarian conferences from 1920 to 1940.

Hawthorne, Nathaniel. Typed manuscript of 1852 excerpt from *American Notebook*.

Jocquith, Abby. "Account of the First Unitarian Meeting at the Isles of Shoals, July 1897." Typed transcript of a *Lowell Courier-Citizen* article.

Mills, Mrs. John F. "The Bell." Handwritten manuscript, 1924.

Oceanic Hotel brochures.

Portsmouth Chronicle, "Rev. George Beebe," May 25, 1856; Star Island land acquisition article, September 19, 1872; "Burning of the First Oceanic Hotel," November 12, 1875; "Old Parsonage," July 1, 1884; Oceanic Hotel advertisement, July 18,1902.

Portsmouth Evening Times. Samuel Caswell hotel article, May 14, 1868.

Tallman, Louise."Faith of Our Fathers: Gosport, 1729 by Rev. Nathaniel Morril, First Minister of Rye." Mimeographed booklet, 1975.

Tallman, Louise H. "Some of the Families of Gosport at the Isles of Shoals, 1715–1876. Compiled from the Church and Town Records of Gosport & Other Sources." Typed manuscript, 1969.

The Lyman V. Rutledge Scrapbook.

The Seventh Annual Report of the Directors of the Society for Promoting Religious Instruction at the Isles of Shoals. November 1829.

The Third Annual Report of the Directors of the Society for Promoting Religious Instruction at the Isles of Shoals. November 1824.

Documents from the Internet

Brewster, Charles W. "Brewster's Rambles About Portsmouth." Portsmouth newspaper columns of the mid-1800s, SeacoastNH.com. 1999.

Cayton, Marie Kuplec. "Who were the evangelicals? Conservative and liberal identity in the Unitarian Controversy in Boston, 1804–1833." *Journal of Social History,* fall 1997.

Finseth, Ian Frederick." 'Liquid Fire Within Me:' Language, Self and Society in Transcendentalism and Early Evangelicalism, 1820-1860." 1995.

Gould, Elizabeth Porter. "Reuben Tracy's Vacation Trips" in *The Bay State Monthly, A Massachusetts Magazine of Literature, History, Biography, and State Progress.* Vol 1, January 1884, a Project Gutenberg eBook.

Greene, Evarts Boutelle. "The Anglican Outlook on the American Colonies in the Early Eighteenth Century" in *American Historical Review,* 64-85. 1914.

Haslett, Charles A. *History of Rockingham County, New Hampshire.* 1915.

Select Committee of the Society for Propagating the Gospel Among the Indians and Others of North America. Annual Reports for 1843, 1844, 1846, 1847, and 1848.

Society for Propagating the Gospel Among Indians and Others in North America. "Brief Account." 1798.

The Star Island Corporation. "Vision 2000: Charting the Future Direction of Star Island, A Mid-Course Adjustment of our Strategic Plan." 2003.

Wilbur, Earl Morse. *Our Unitarian Heritage.* 1925.